EASY PIANO

FAVORITE SONGS
IN EASY KEYS

"Favorite Songs in Easy Keys" include⬚⬚⬚⬚⬚e flat in the **key signature**.
The key signature appears on t⬚⬚⬚⬚⬚⬚ext to the clef signs.

no sharps or flats

one sharp: F#
all Fs are played as F#

one flat: B♭
all Bs are played as B♭

Sometimes **accidentals** appear. Accidentals are sharps and flats not in the key signature.
An accidental alters a specific note in a particular measure. The next bar line or a
natural sign (♮) cancels an accidental.

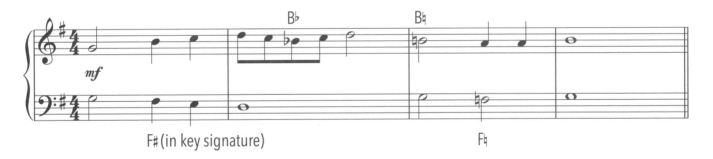

F# (in key signature)

ISBN 978-1-70514-257-8

HAL•LEONARD®
7777 W. BLUEMOUND RD. P.O. BOX 13819 MILWAUKEE, WI 53213

Visit Hal Leonard Online at
www.halleonard.com

Contact us:
Hal Leonard
7777 West Bluemound Road
Milwaukee, WI 53213
Email: info@halleonard.com

In Europe, contact:
Hal Leonard Europe Limited
42 Wigmore Street
Marylebone, London, W1U 2RN
Email: info@halleonardeurope.com

In Australia, contact:
Hal Leonard Australia Pty. Ltd.
4 Lentara Court
Cheltenham, Victoria, 3192 Australia
Email: info@halleonard.com.au

AFRICA

Words and Music by DAVID PAICH
and JEFF PORCARO

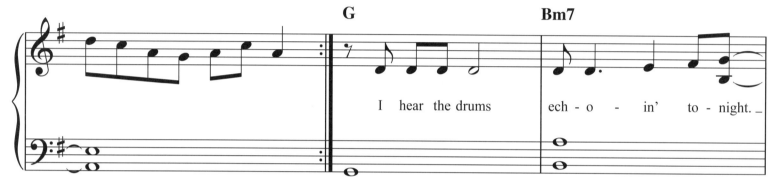

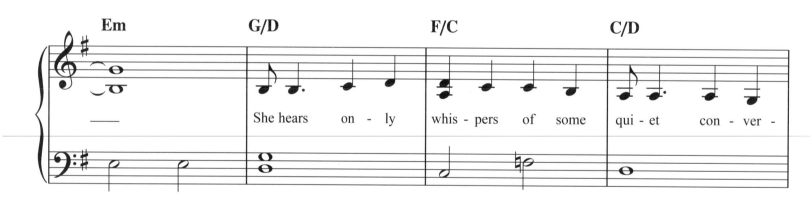

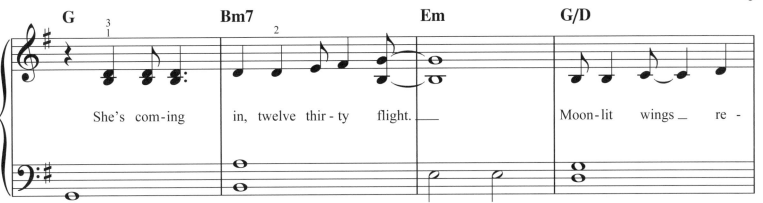

She's com-ing in, twelve thir-ty flight. ___ Moon-lit wings ___ re-

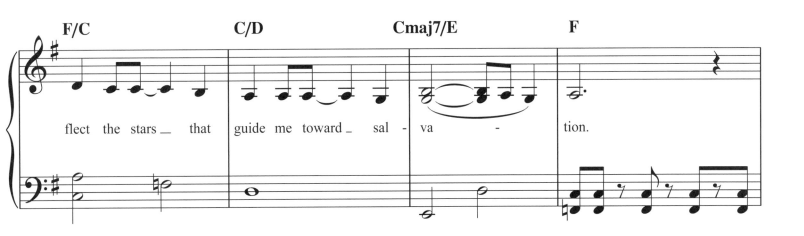

flect the stars ___ that guide me toward ___ sal - va - tion.

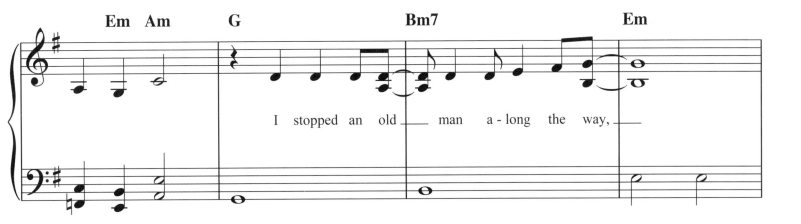

I stopped an old ___ man a-long the way, ___

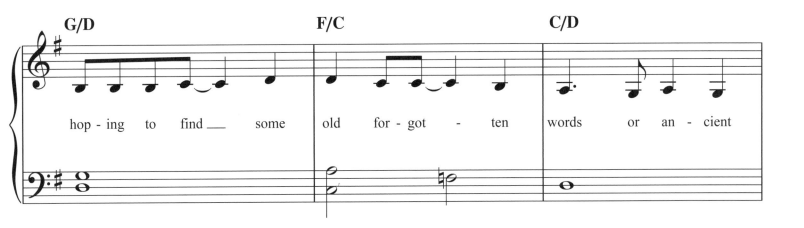

hop-ing to find ___ some old for-got - ten words or an - cient

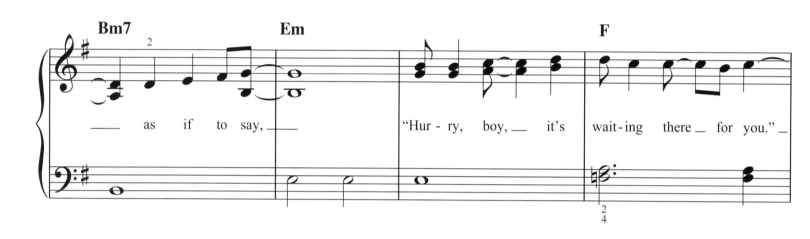

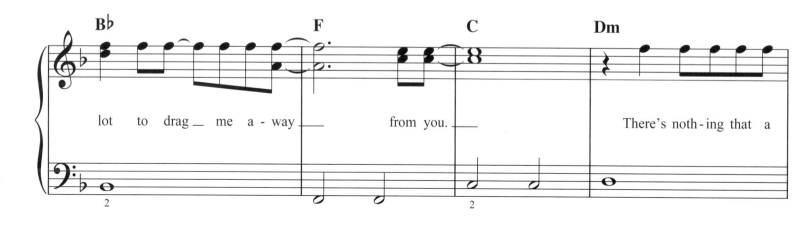

hun-dred men __ or more __ could ev - er do. __ I bless the rains __

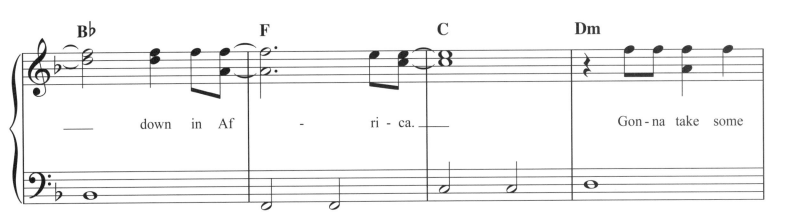

__ down in Af - ri - ca. __ Gon - na take some

time to do __ the things we nev - er had. __

ALL OF ME

Words and Music by JOHN STEPHENS
and TOBY GAD

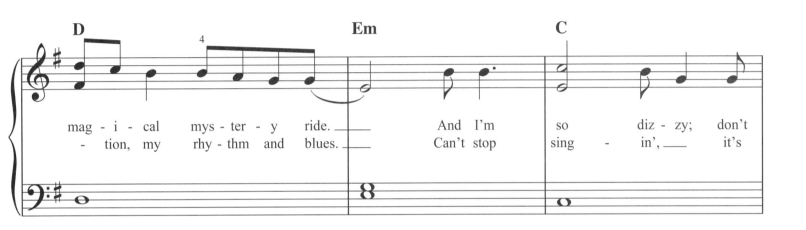

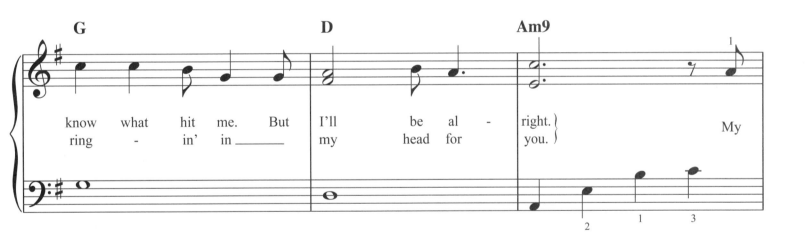

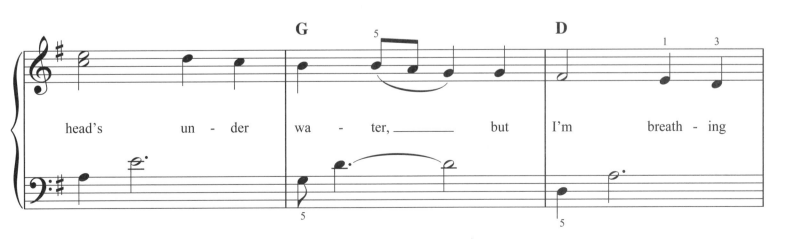

10

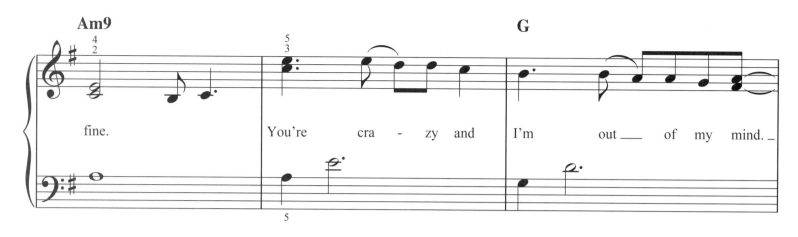

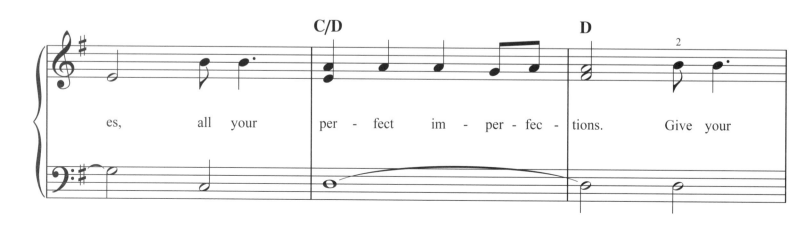

11

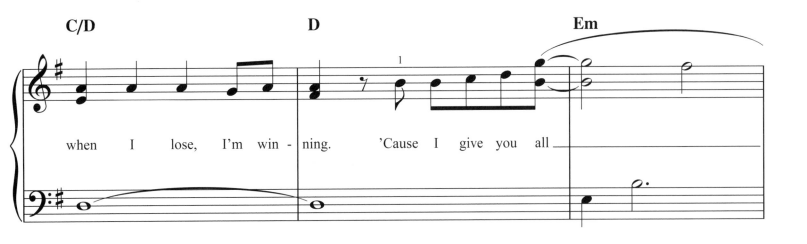

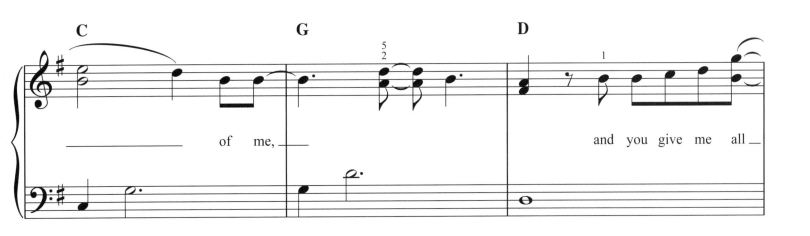

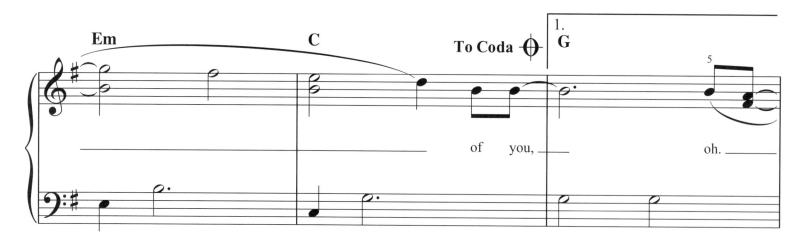

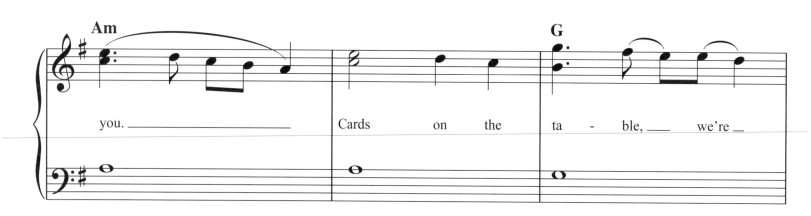

BABY LOVE

Words and Music by BRIAN HOLLAND,
EDWARD HOLLAND JR. and LAMONT DOZIER

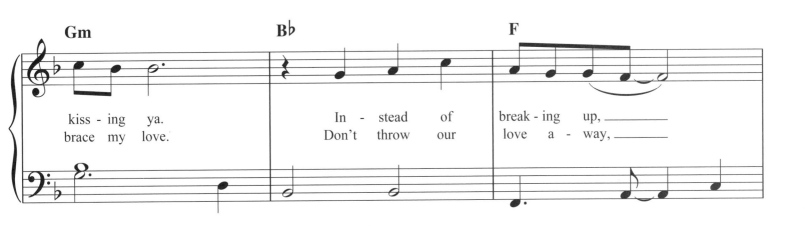

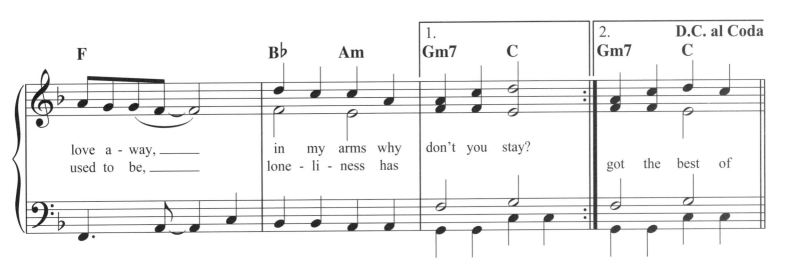

CODA

F   Cm/E♭   D7

hurt me,   'till it   hurt me.   Ooh, ____

Gm7   B♭   F

ba - by love.   Don't throw our   love a - way,

B♭   F

don't throw our   love a - way.

Additional Lyrics

3. Got the best of me, my love, my baby love
   I need ya, oh, how I need ya. Why you do me
   Like you do, after I've been true to you?
   So deep in love with you. Baby, baby.
   Ooh. 'Til it hurt me, 'til it hurt me.

ALL YOU NEED IS LOVE

Words and Music by JOHN LENNON
and PAUL McCARTNEY

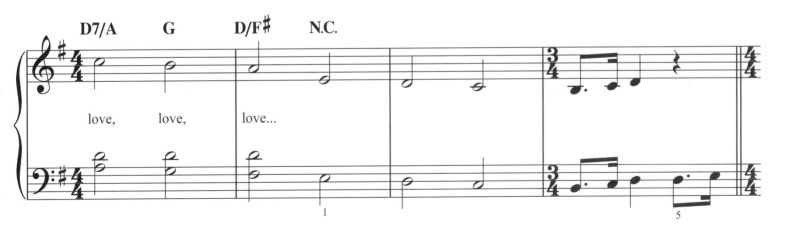

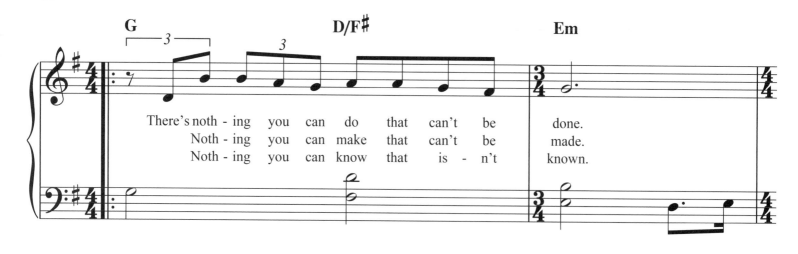

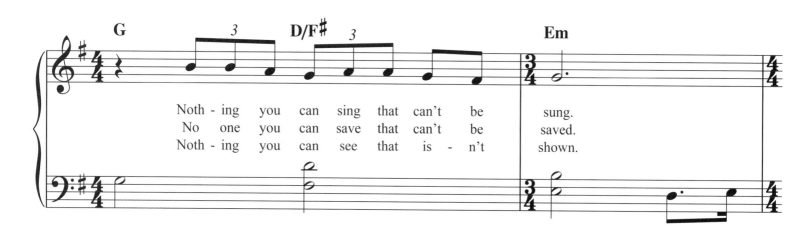

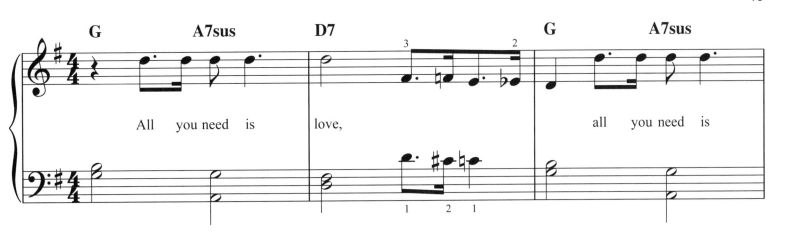

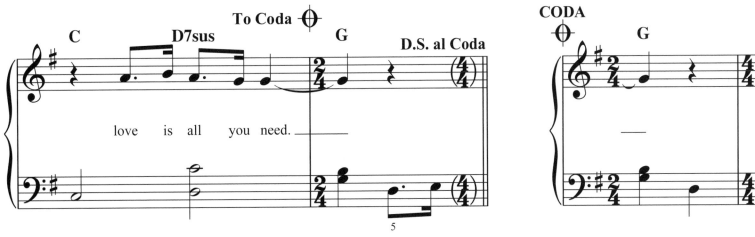
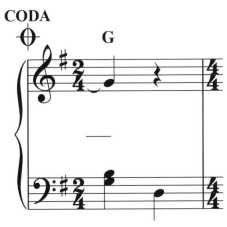

BOHEMIAN RHAPSODY

Words and Music by
FREDDIE MERCURY

Slowly

Ma - ma _____ just
Too late, _____ my

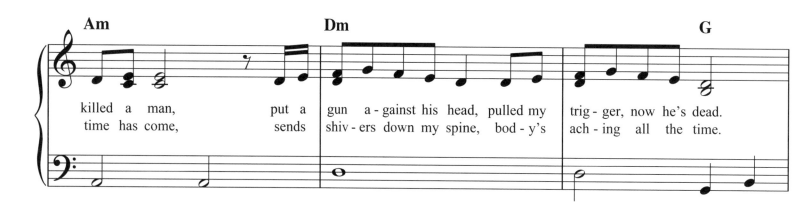

killed a man, put a gun a - gainst his head, pulled my trig - ger, now he's dead.
time has come, sends shiv - ers down my spine, bod - y's ach - ing all the time.

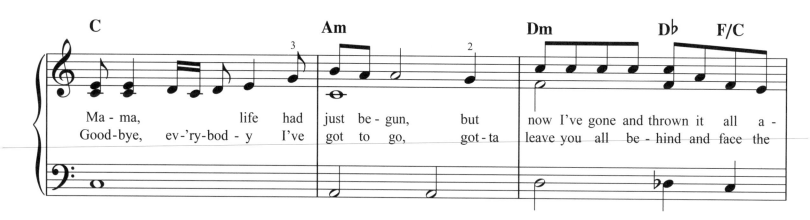

Ma - ma, life had just be - gun, but now I've gone and thrown it all a -
Good-bye, ev - 'ry - bod - y I've got to go, got - ta leave you all be - hind and face the

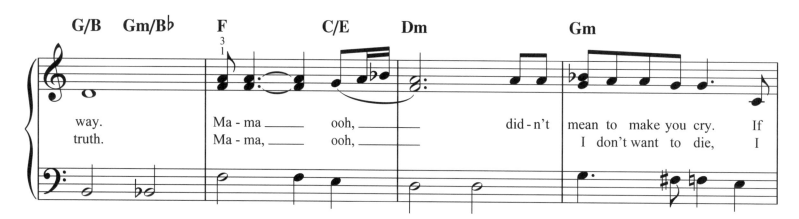

way. Ma - ma _____ ooh, did - n't mean to make you cry. If
truth. Ma - ma, _____ ooh, _____ I don't want to die, I

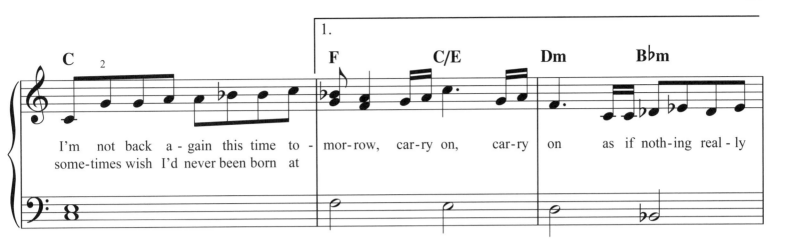

I'm not back a - gain this time to - mor-row, car-ry on, car-ry on as if noth-ing real - ly
some-times wish I'd never been born at

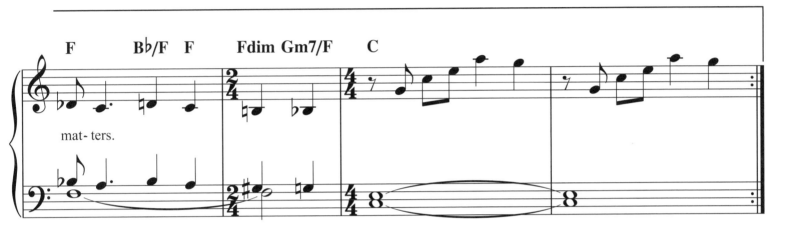

mat- ters.

all.

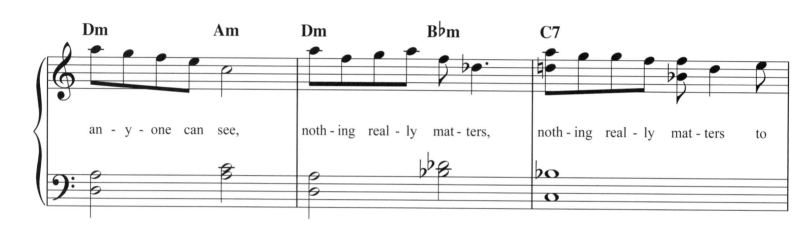

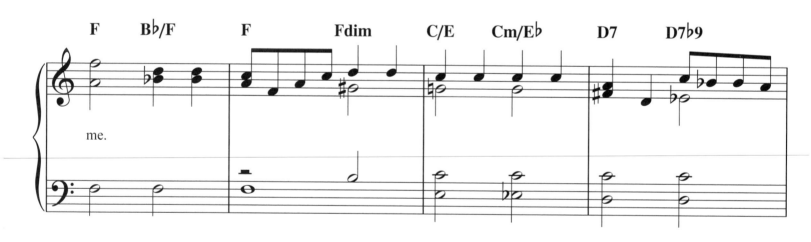

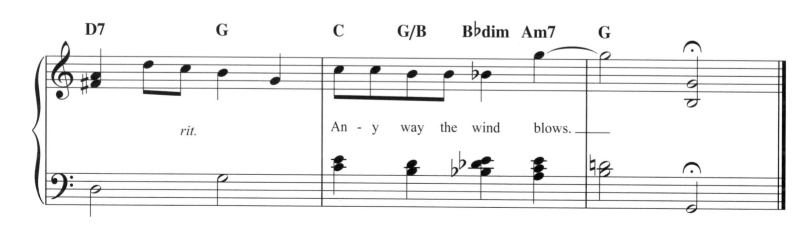

BLUE SKIES
from BETSY

Words and Music by
IRVING BERLIN

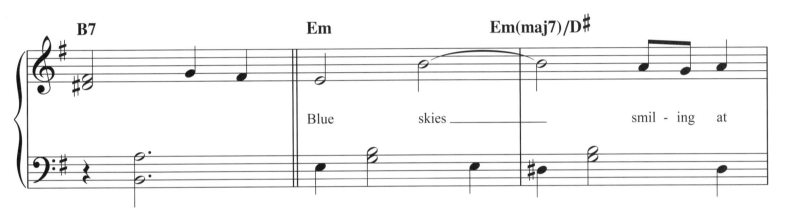

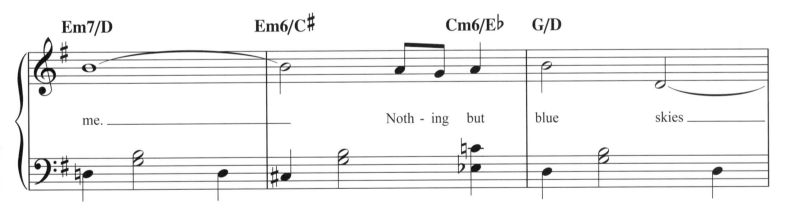

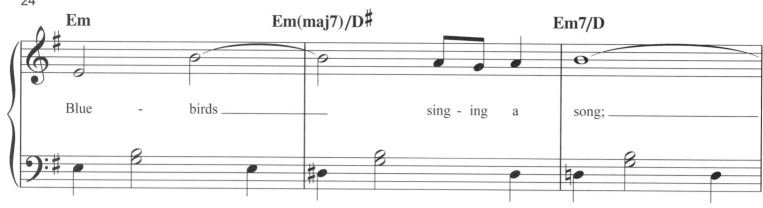

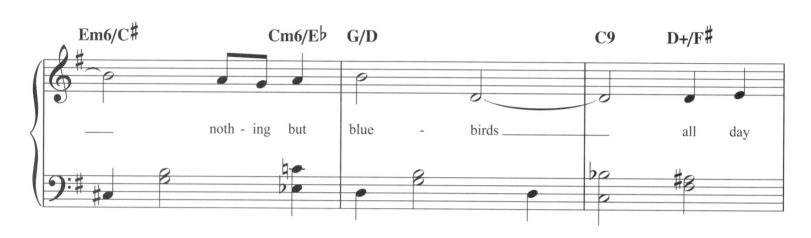

No - tic - ing the days hur - ry - ing by; when you're in love,

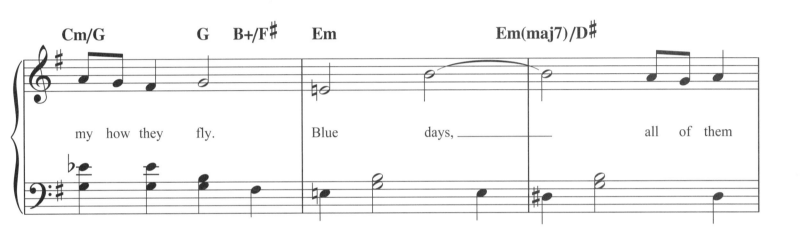

my how they fly. Blue days,_____ all of them

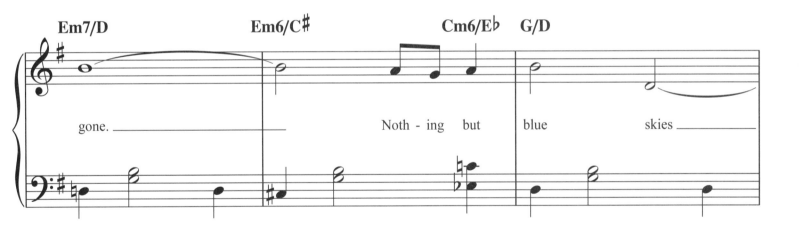

gone. _____ Noth - ing but blue skies _____

_____ from now on.

CROCODILE ROCK

Words and Music by ELTON JOHN
and BERNIE TAUPIN

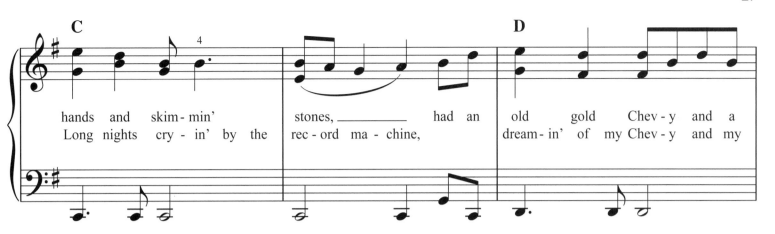

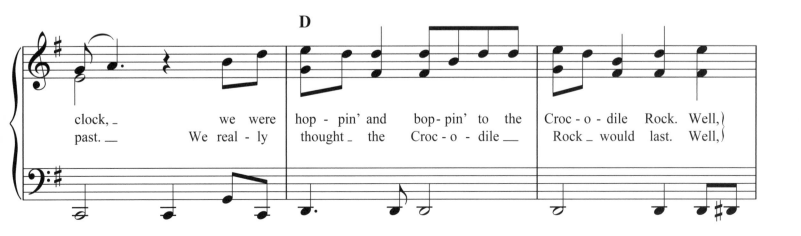

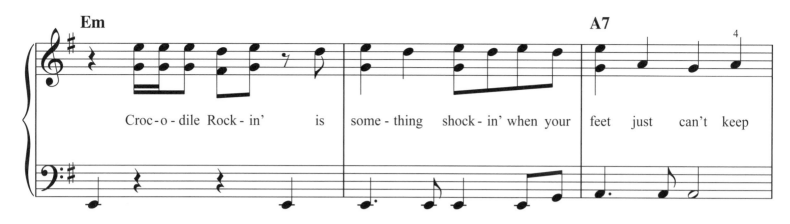

DANCING QUEEN

Words and Music by BENNY ANDERSSON,
BJÖRN ULVAEUS and STIG ANDERSON

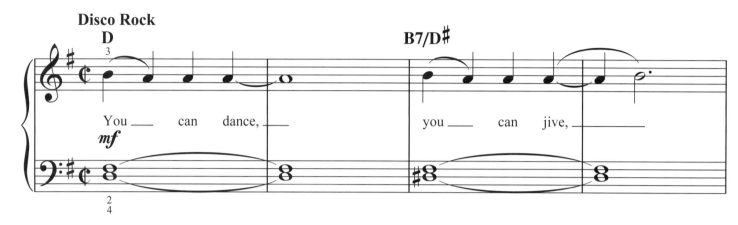

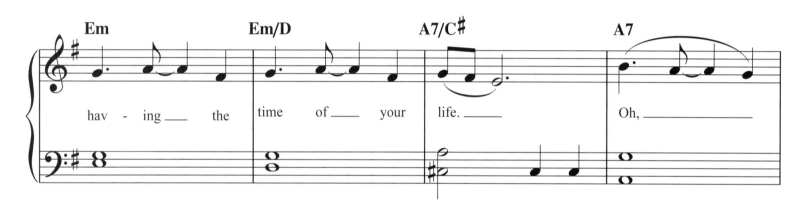

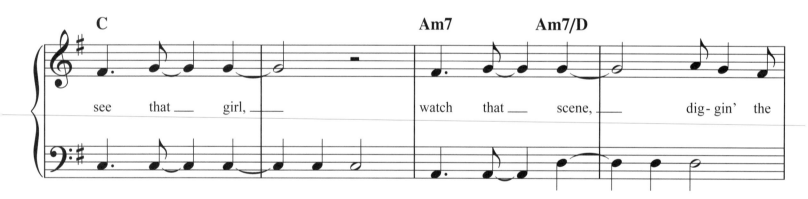

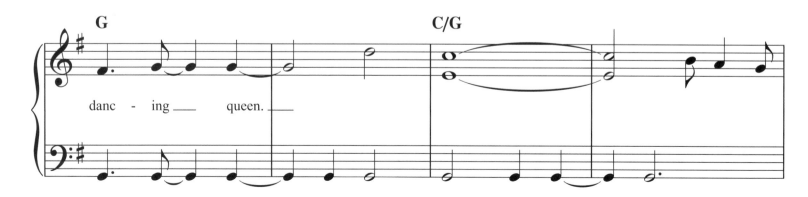

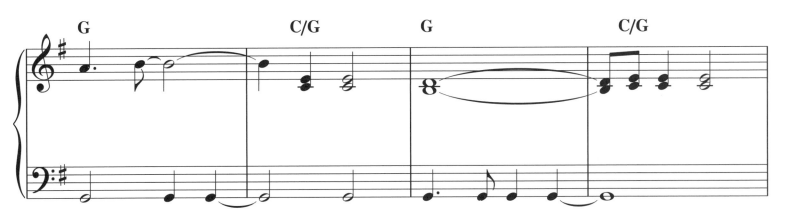

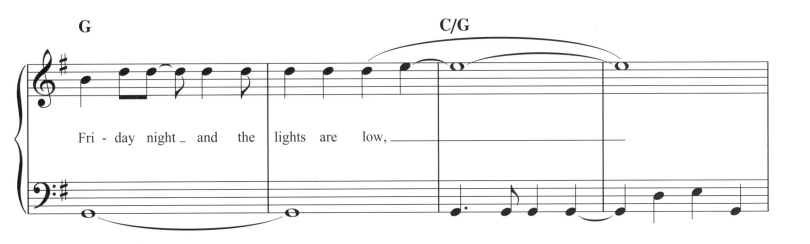

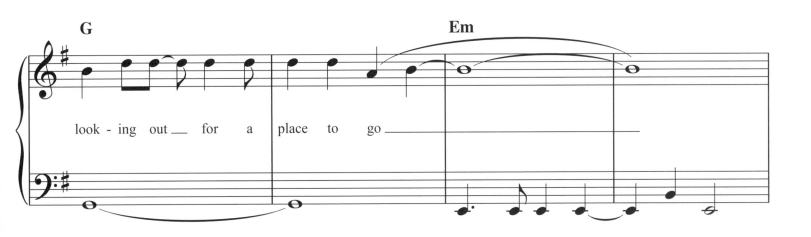

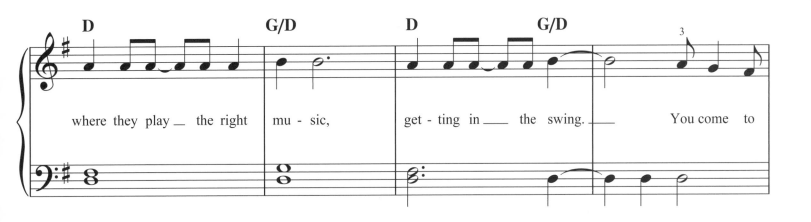

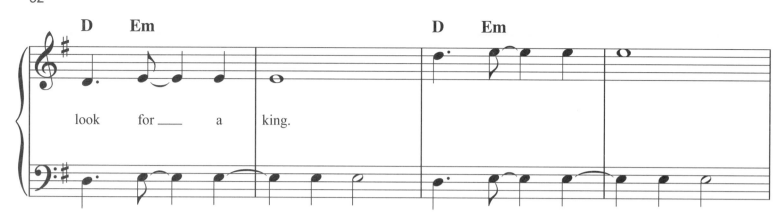

look for ___ a king.

An - y - bod - y could be that guy. ___

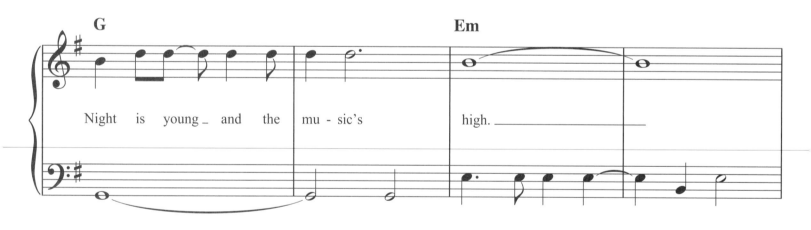

Night is young ___ and the mu - sic's high. ___

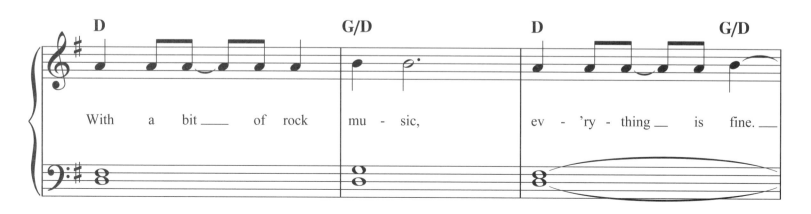

With a bit ___ of rock mu - sic, ev - 'ry - thing ___ is fine. ___

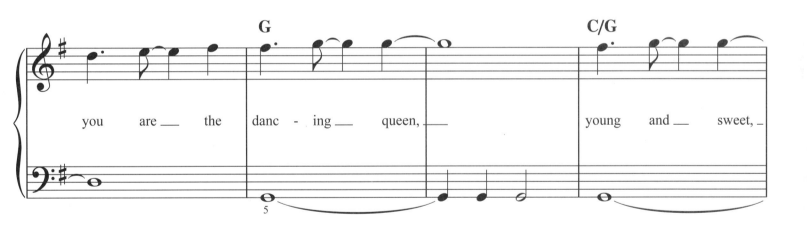

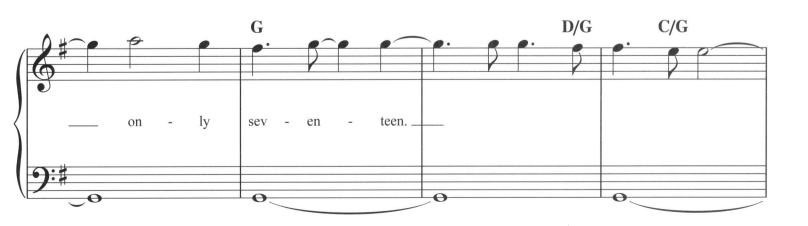

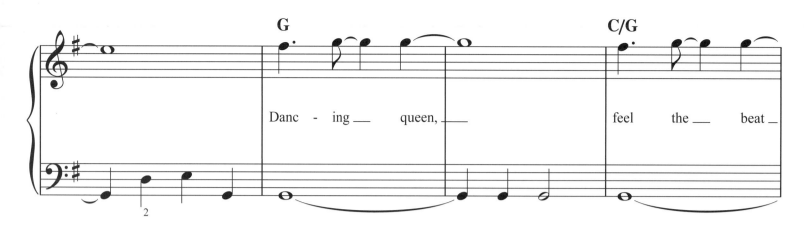

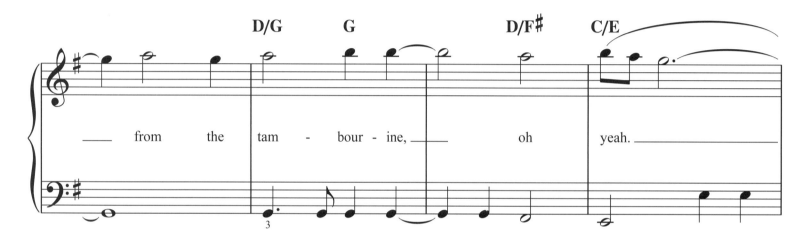

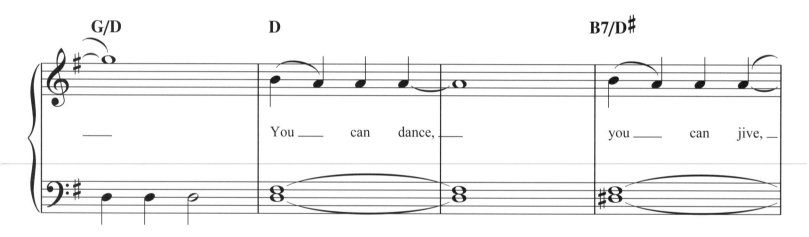

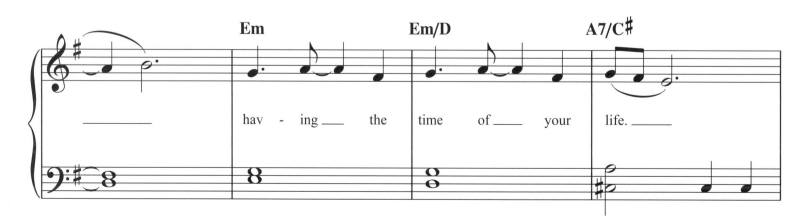

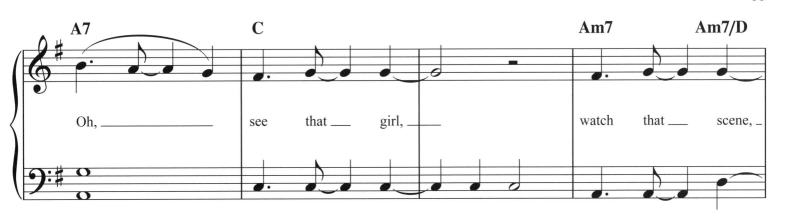

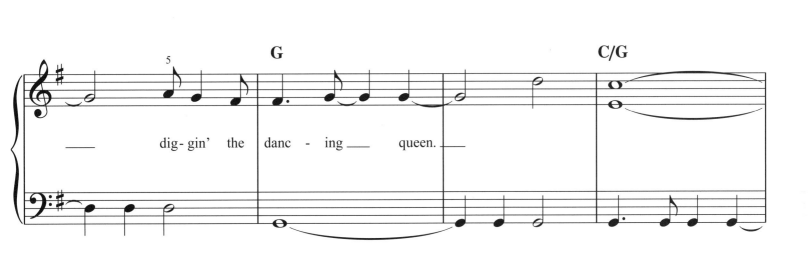

I WILL ALWAYS LOVE YOU

Words and Music by
DOLLY PARTON

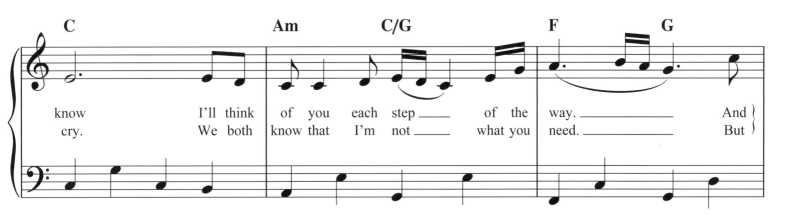

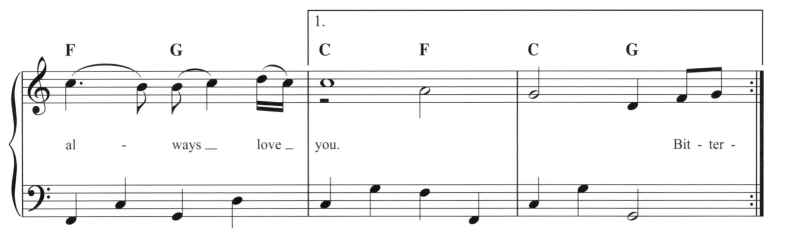

JOLENE

Words and Music by
DOLLY PARTON

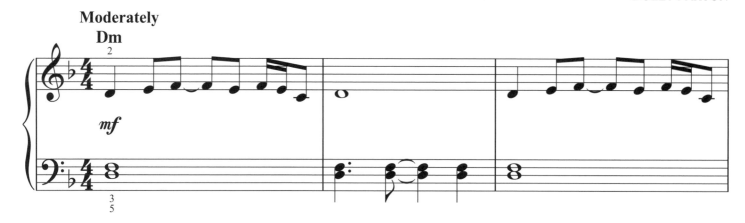

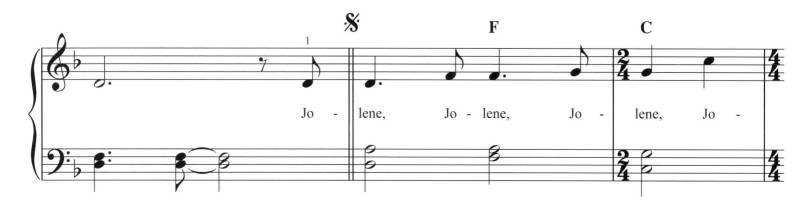

Jo - lene, Jo - lene, Jo - lene, Jo -

lene, _____ I'm beg-ging of you please don't take my man. _____

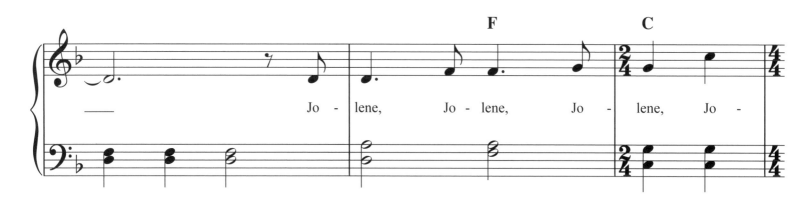

_____ Jo - lene, Jo - lene, Jo - lene, Jo -

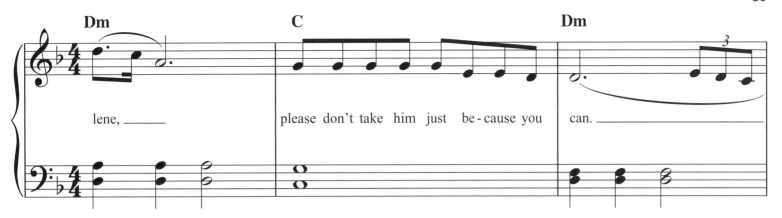

lene, _____ please don't take him just be-cause you can. _____

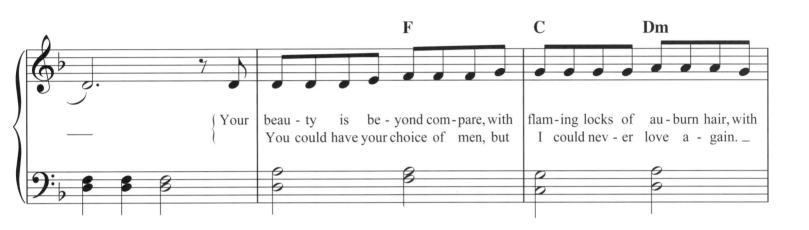

_____ { Your beau - ty is be - yond com - pare, with
You could have your choice of men, but flam-ing locks of au - burn hair, with
I could nev - er love a - gain. _

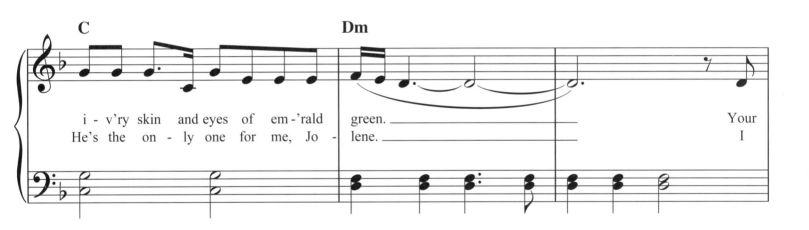

i - v'ry skin and eyes of em -'rald green. _____ Your
He's the on - ly one for me, Jo - lene. _____ I

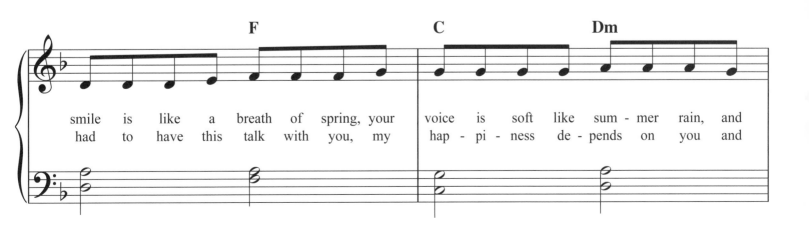

smile is like a breath of spring, your voice is soft like sum - mer rain, and
had to have this talk with you, my hap - pi - ness de - pends on you and

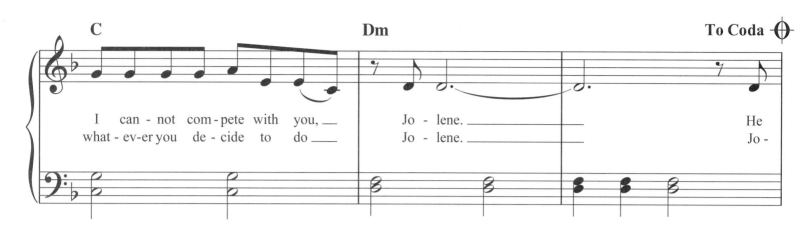

To Coda

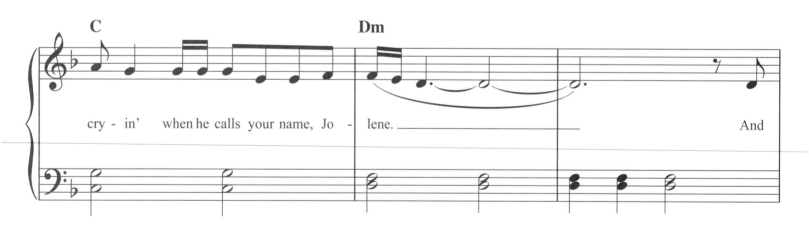

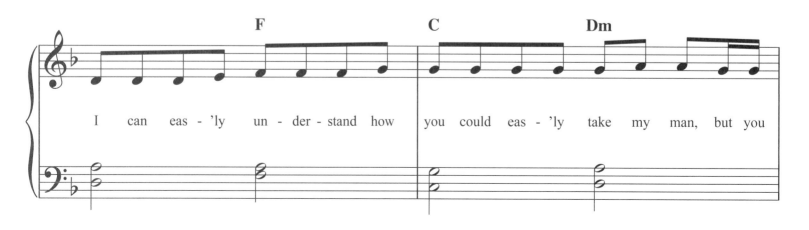

D.S. al Coda

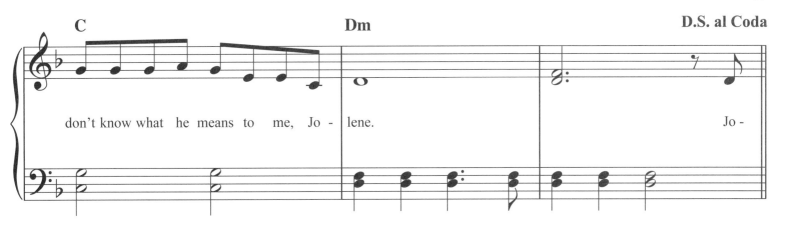

don't know what he means to me, Jo - lene. Jo -

CODA

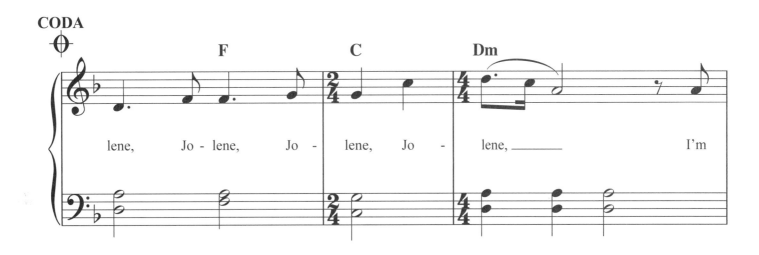

lene, Jo - lene, Jo - lene, Jo - lene, _____ I'm

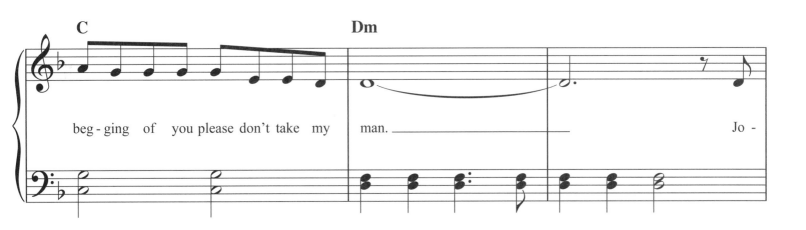

beg - ging of you please don't take my man. _____ Jo -

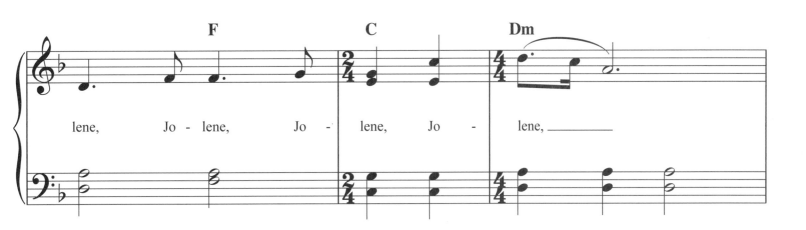

lene, Jo - lene, Jo - lene, Jo - lene, _____

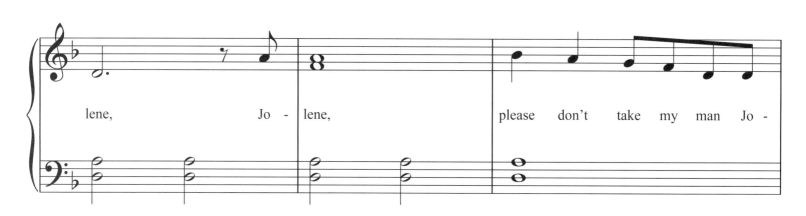

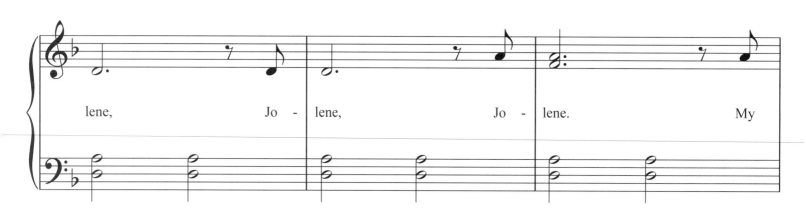

MRS. ROBINSON

Words and Music by
PAUL SIMON

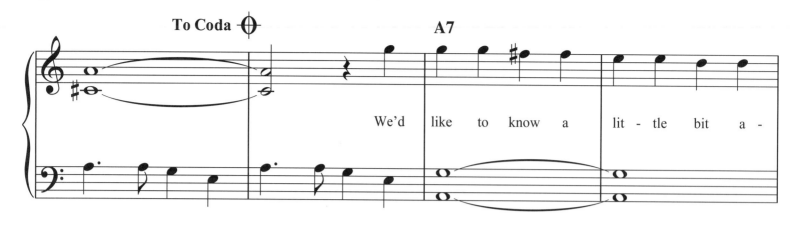

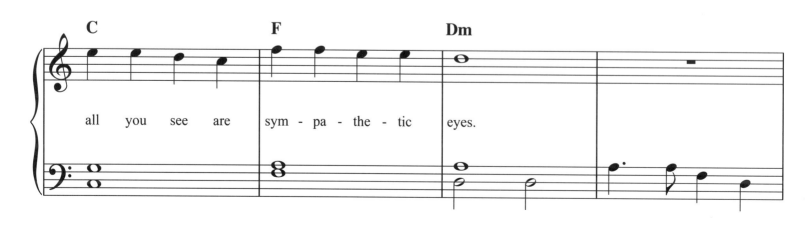

D.S. al Coda
(with repeat)

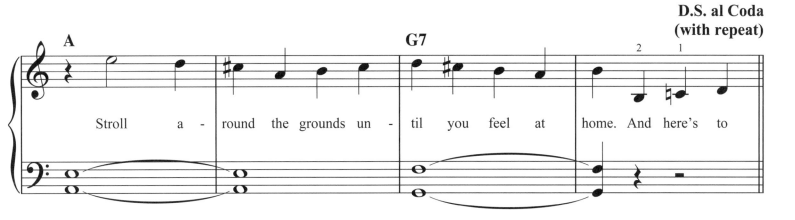

Stroll a - round the grounds un - til you feel at home. And here's to

CODA

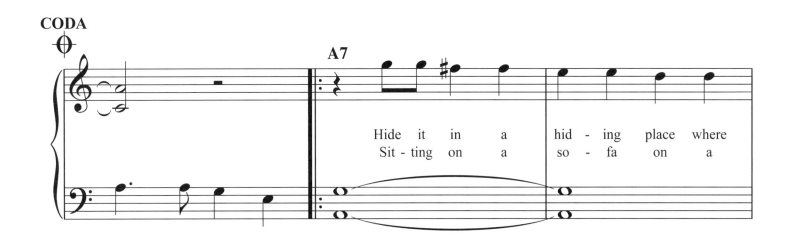

Hide it in a hid - ing place where
Sit - ting on a so - fa on a

no one ev - er goes, put it in your
Sun - day af - ter - noon, go - ing to the

pan - try with your cup - cakes. It's a lit - tle
can - di - date's de - bate. Laugh a - bout it,

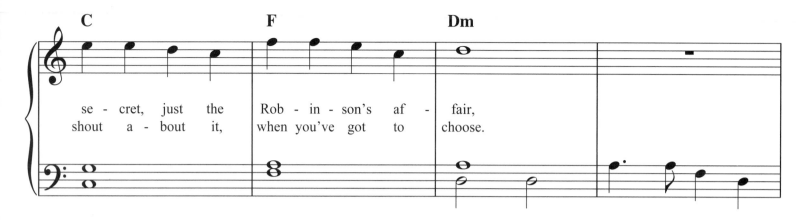

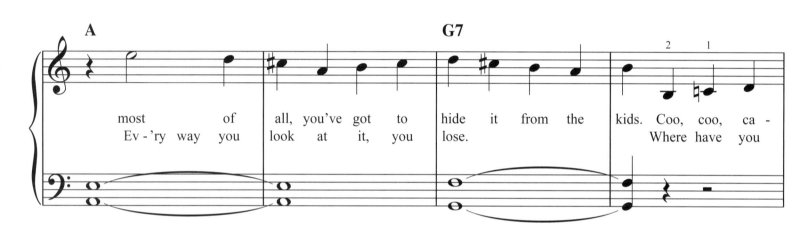

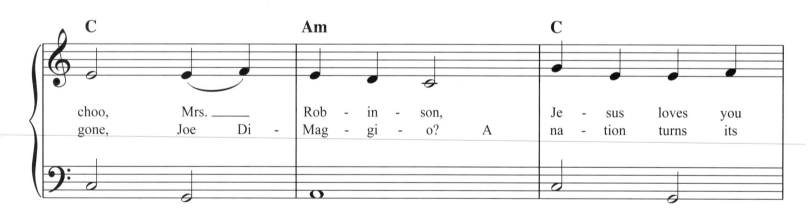

God bless you, please, Mrs. ____ Rob - in - son,
What's that you say, Mrs. ____ Rob - in - son,

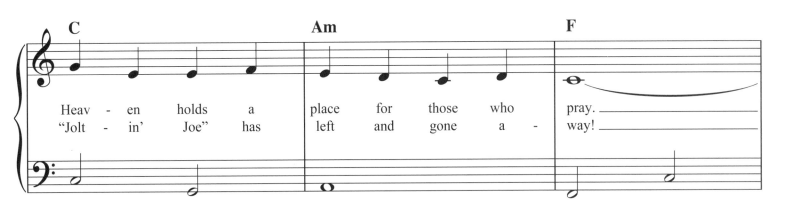

Heav - en holds a place for those who pray. ____
"Jolt - in' Joe" has left and gone a - way! ____

____ (Hey, hey, hey, ____ hey, hey, hey.)
____ (Hey, hey, hey, ____ hey, hey, hey.)

JUST THE WAY YOU ARE

Words and Music by
BILLY JOEL

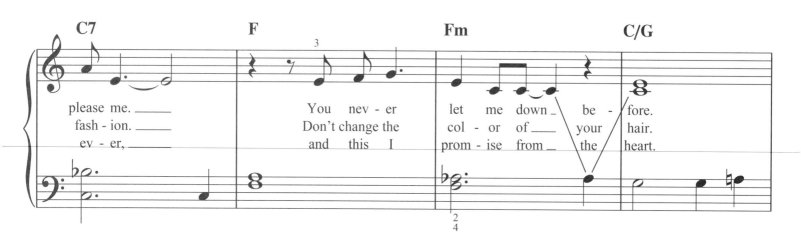

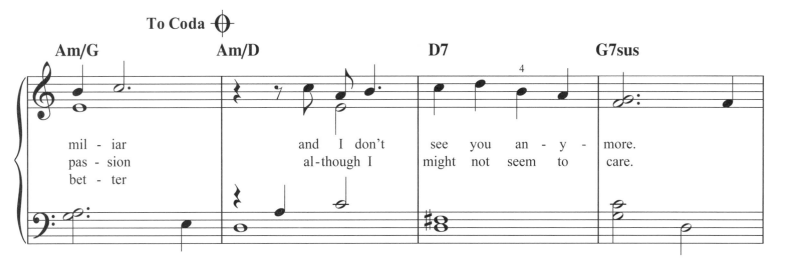

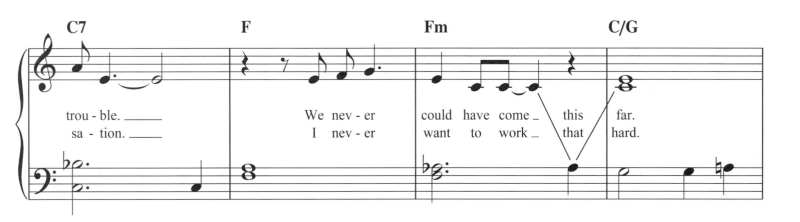

bad times.
talk to.
I'll take you
I want you
just the way ___ you are.
just the way ___ you are.

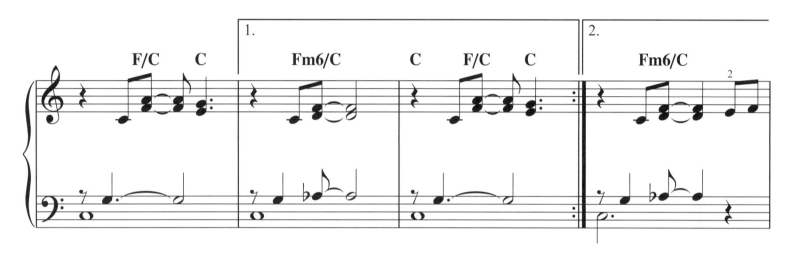

I need to know that you will al - ways

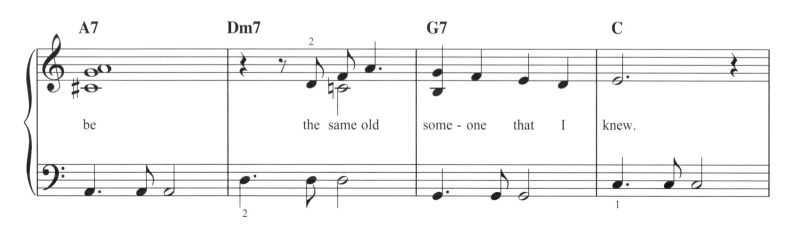

be
the same old
some - one that I
knew.

Oh! What will it take 'til you be - lieve in

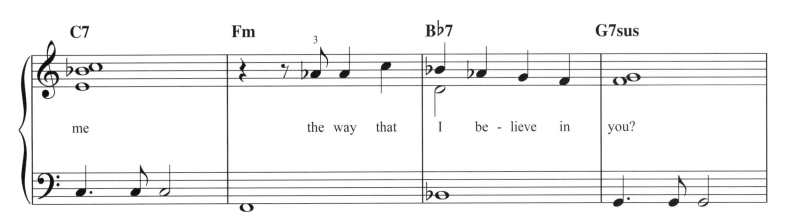

me the way that I be - lieve in you?

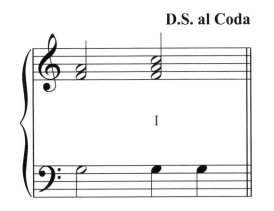

I

I want you just the way you

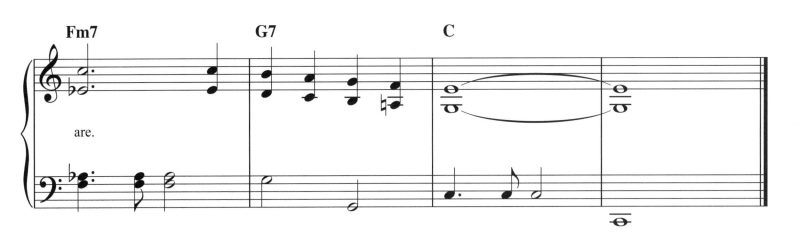

are.

OCTOPUS'S GARDEN

Words and Music by
RICHARD STARKEY

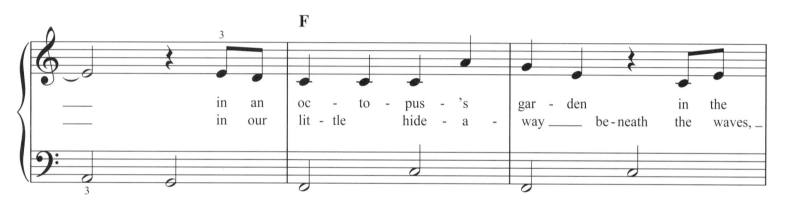

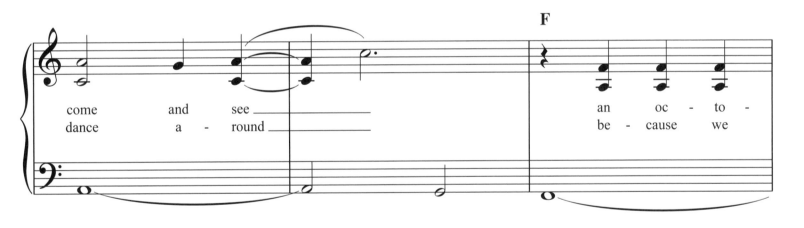

I'd like to be _____ un – der the sea _____

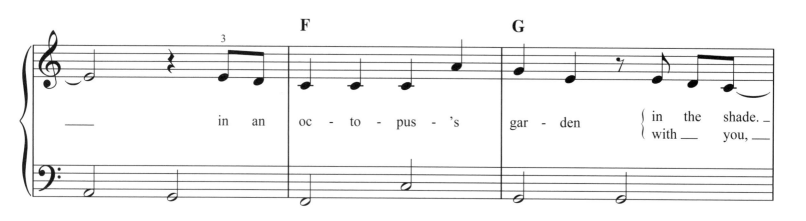

_____ in an oc – to – pus – 's gar – den { in the shade. _____
{ with _____ you, _____

1. 2.

in an oc – to – pus – 's

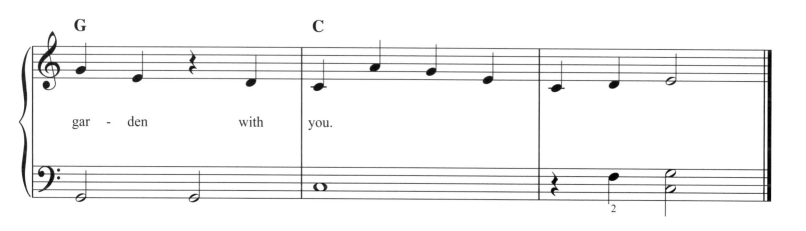

gar – den with you.

MY GIRL

Words and Music by SMOKEY ROBINSON
and RONALD WHITE

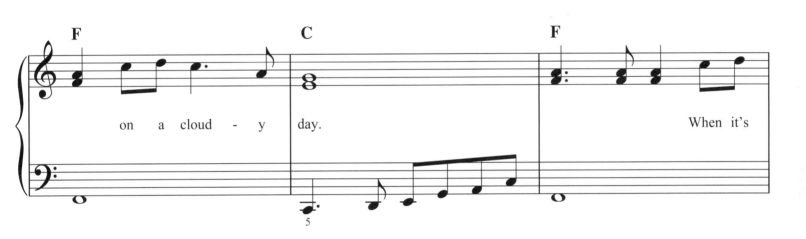

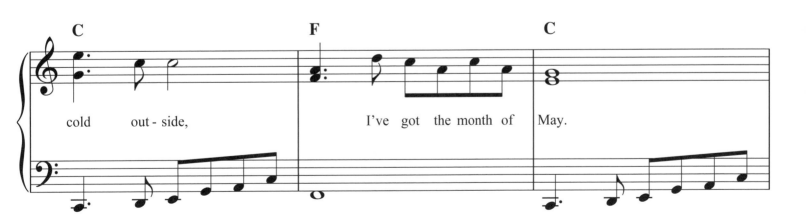

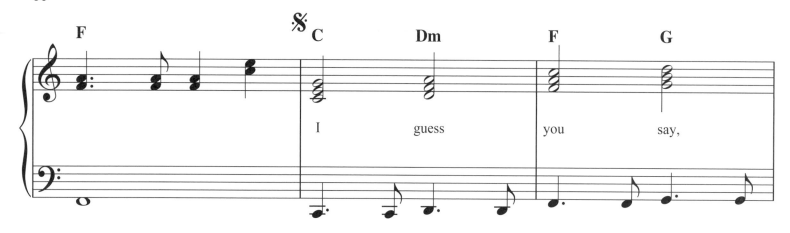

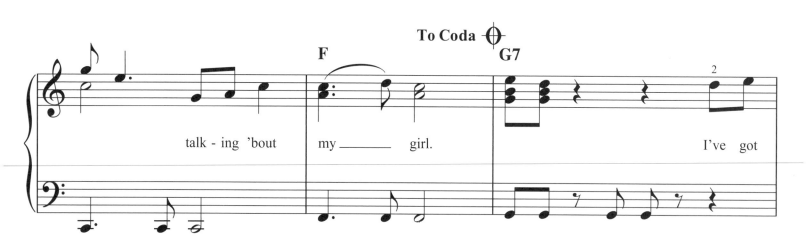

I've got a sweet-er song _____ than the birds in the

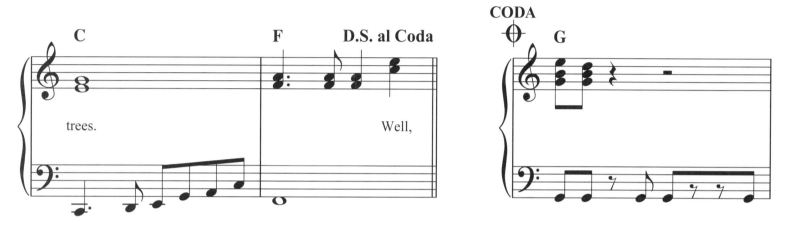

trees. Well,

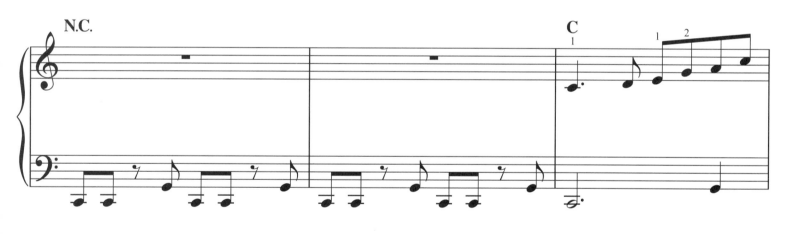

OVER THE RAINBOW
from THE WIZARD OF OZ

Music by HAROLD ARLEN
Lyric by E.Y. "YIP" HARBURG

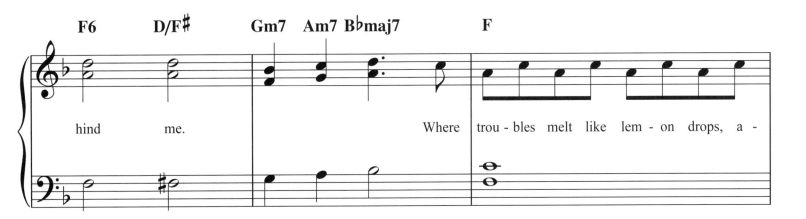

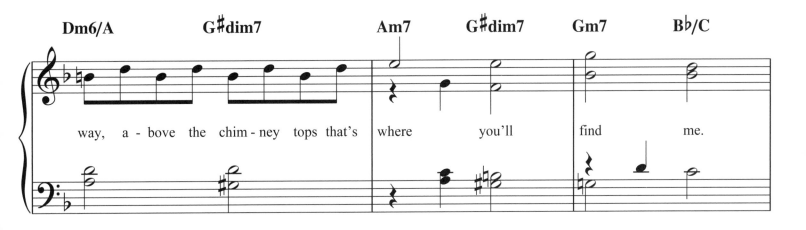

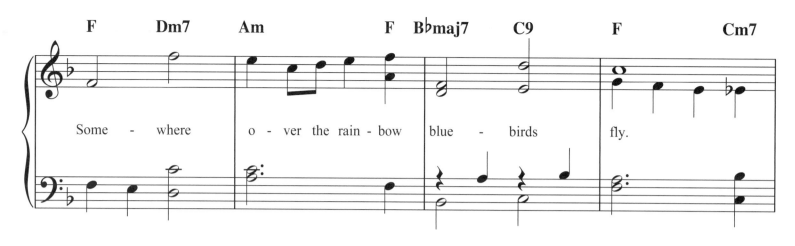

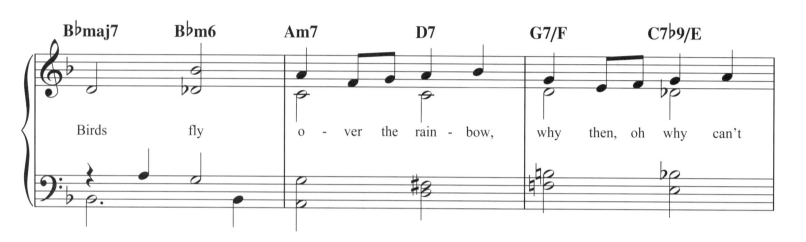

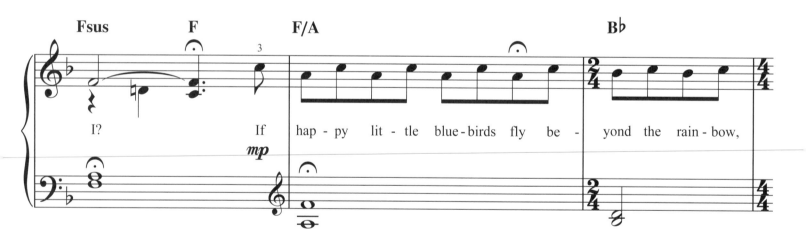

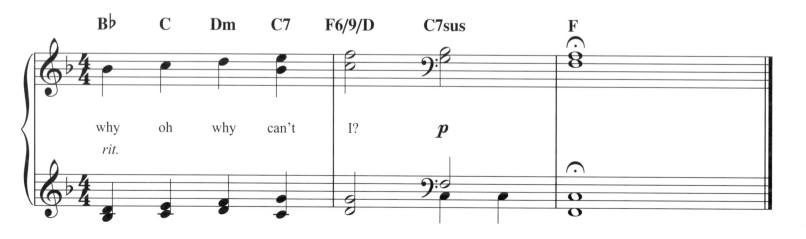

STAND BY ME

Words and Music by JERRY LEIBER,
MIKE STOLLER and BEN E. KING

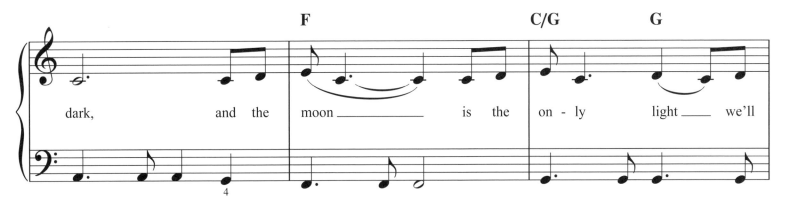

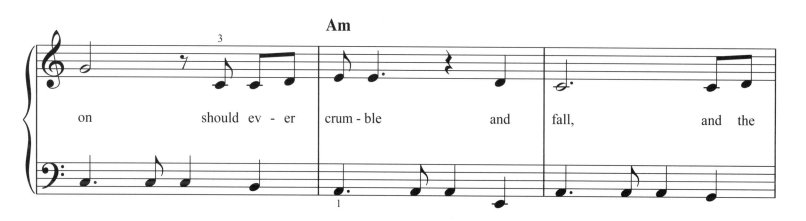

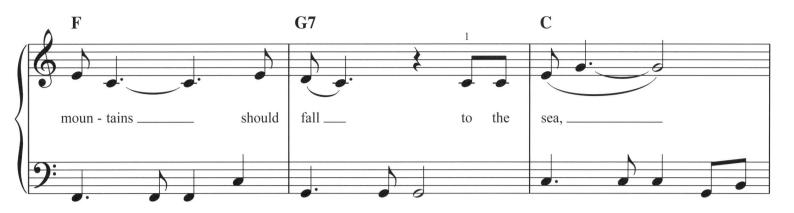

moun - tains _____ should fall ___ to the sea, _____

no, I won't _ be a - fraid, _ no, I won't ___ shed a

tear just as long _ as you stand, _ stand by me.

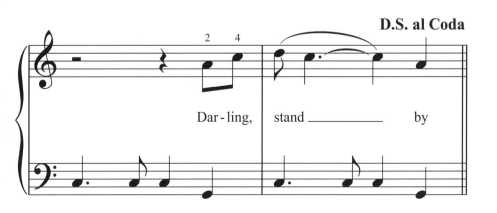

Dar - ling, stand _____ by

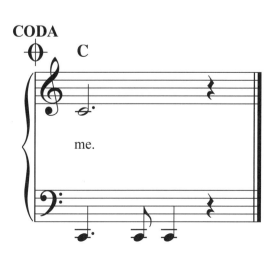

me.

PROUD MARY

Words and Music by
JOHN FOGERTY

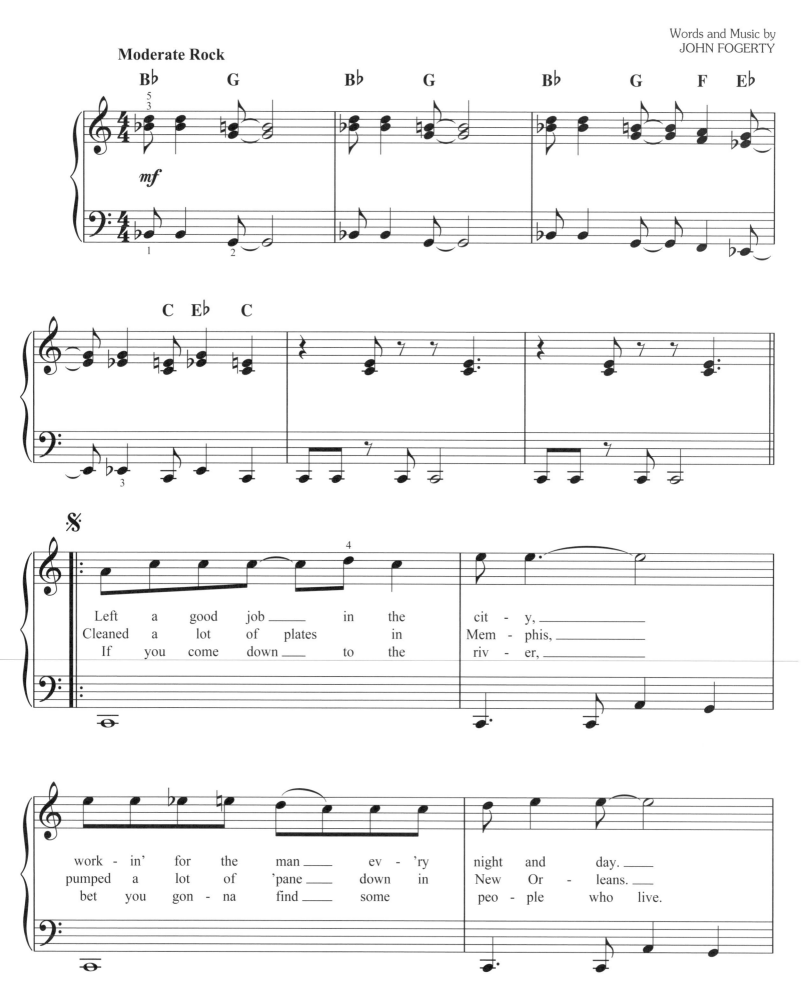

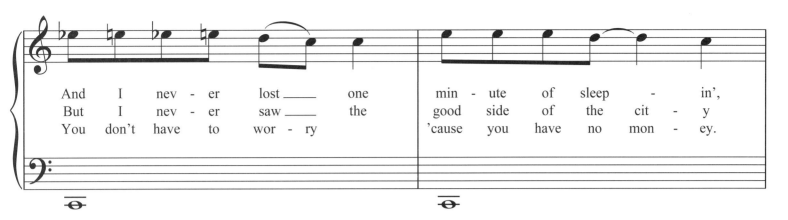

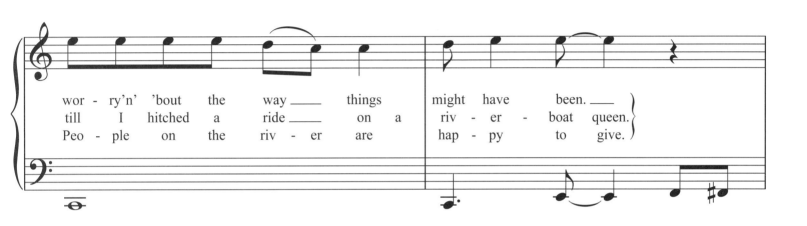

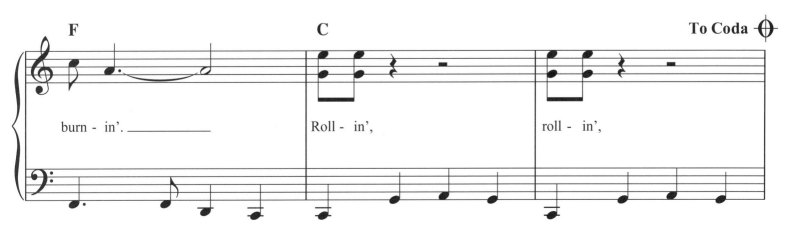

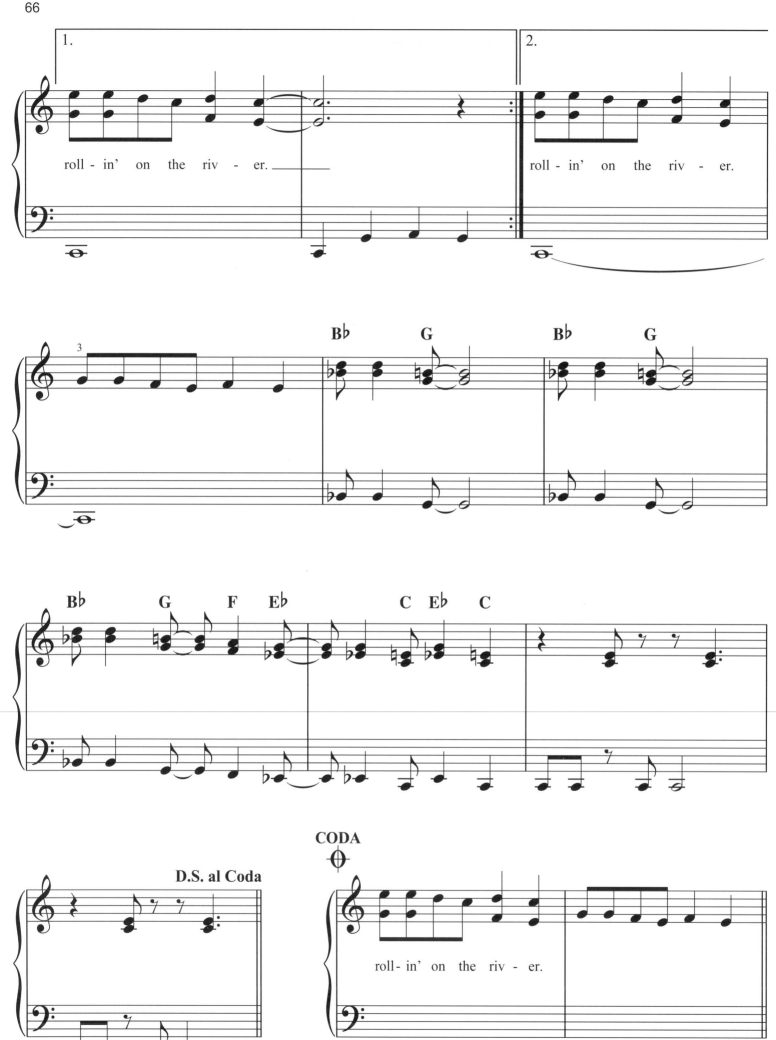

rollin' on the river.

rollin' on the river.

rollin' on the river.

D.S. al Coda

CODA

Roll - in', roll - in', roll - in' on the riv - er. ____

roll - in' on the riv - er.

THE RAINBOW CONNECTION
from THE MUPPET MOVIE

Words and Music by PAUL WILLIAMS
and KENNETH L. ASCHER

Flowing Waltz

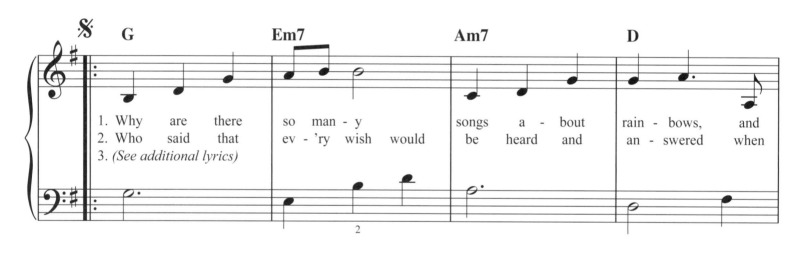

1. Why are there so man - y songs a - bout rain - bows, and
2. Who said that ev - 'ry wish would be heard and an - swered when
3. *(See additional lyrics)*

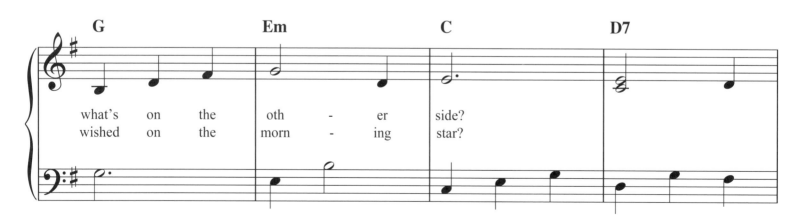

what's on the oth - er side?
wished on the morn - ing star?

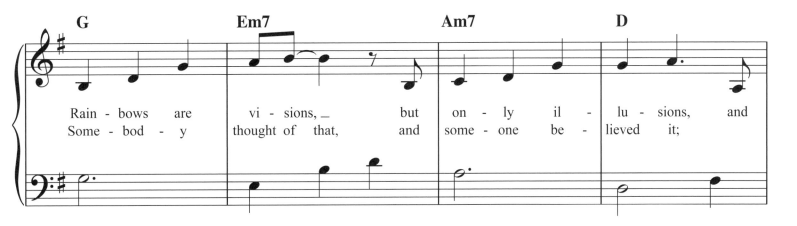

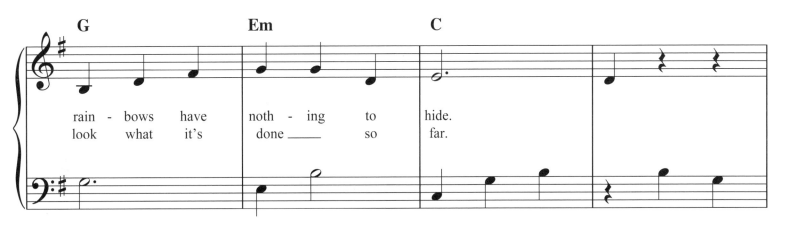

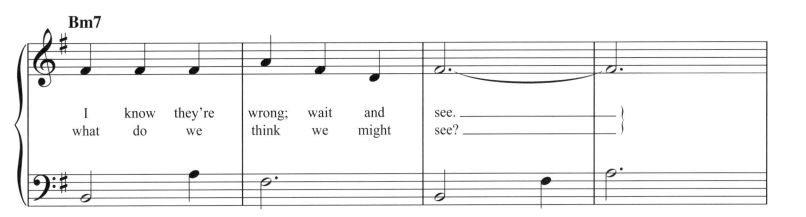

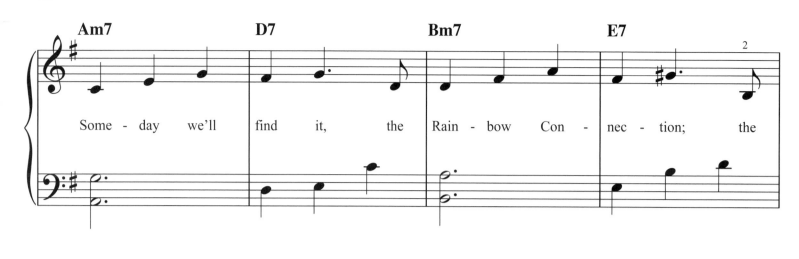

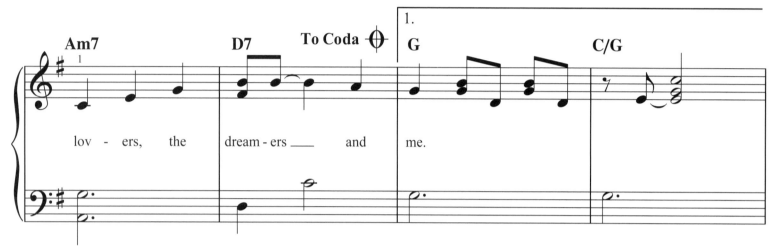

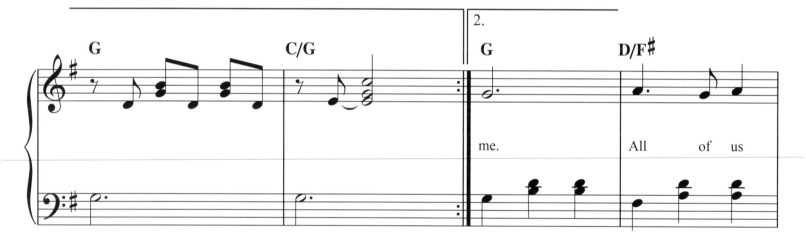

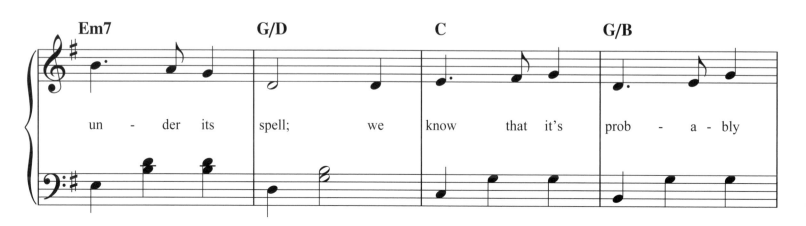

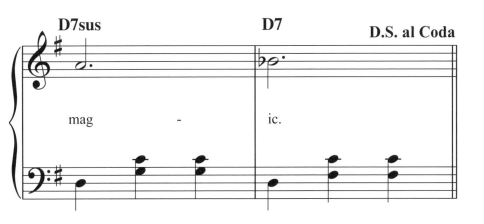
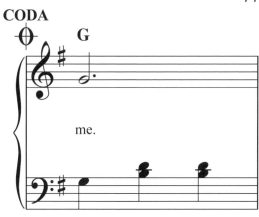
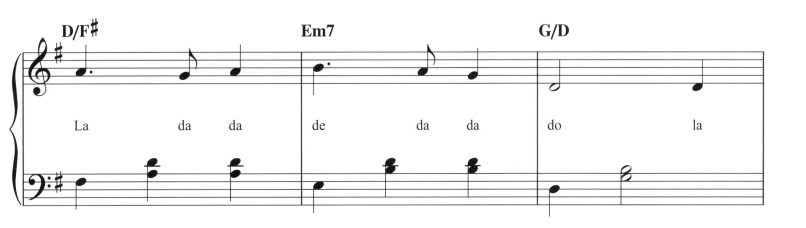
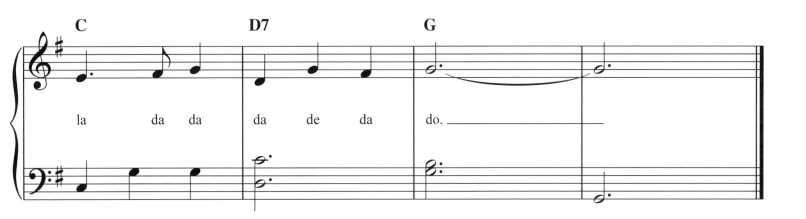

Additional Lyrics

3. Have you been half asleep and have you heard voices?
I've heard them calling my name.
Is this the sweet sound that calls the young sailors?
The voice might be one and the same.
I've heard it too many times to ignore it.
It's something that I'm s'posed to be.
Someday we'll find it,
The Rainbow Connection;
The lovers, the dreamers and me.

SPIRIT IN THE SKY

Words and Music by
NORMAN GREENBAUM

Moderate Rock Shuffle

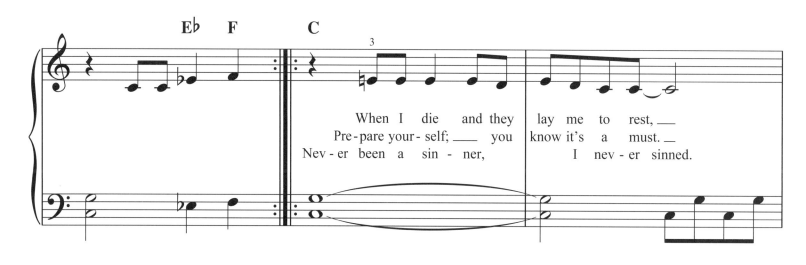

When I die and they lay me to rest, ___
Pre - pare your - self; ___ you know it's a must. ___
Nev - er been a sin - ner, I nev - er sinned.

gon - na go ___ to the place ___ that's the best. ___ When I lay me down ___
Got - ta have a friend in ___ Je - sus, ___ so you know that when ___
I got a friend ___ in ___ Je - sus, ___ so you know that when ___

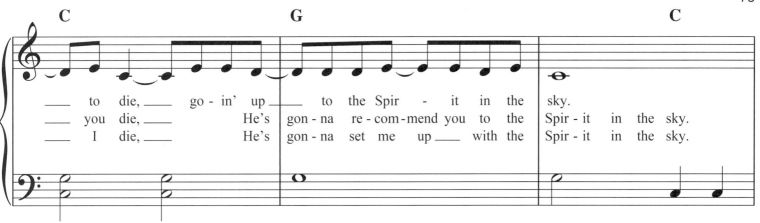

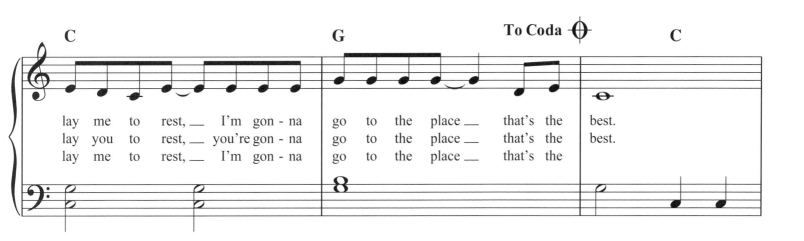

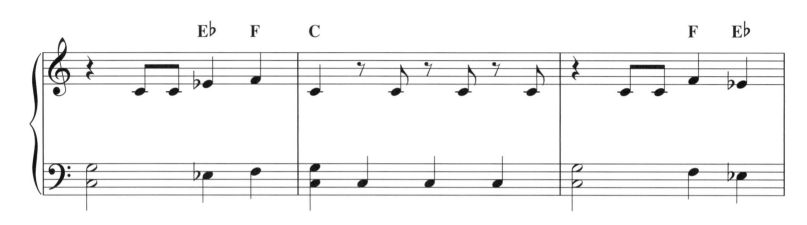

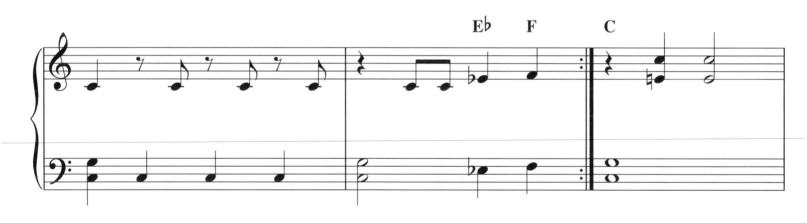

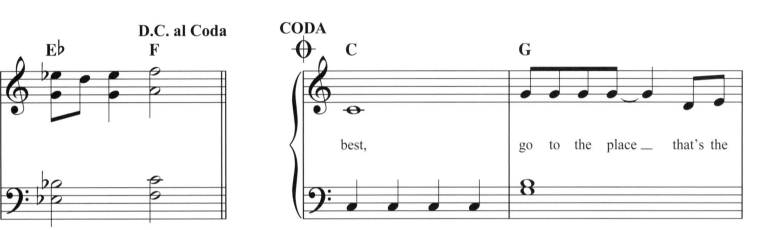

SWEET HOME ALABAMA

Words and Music by RONNIE VAN ZANT,
ED KING and GARY ROSSINGTON

Moderately slow

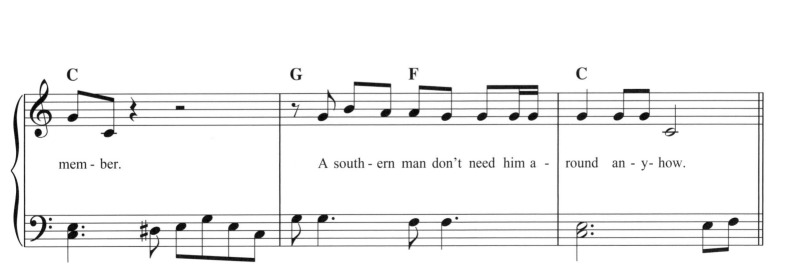

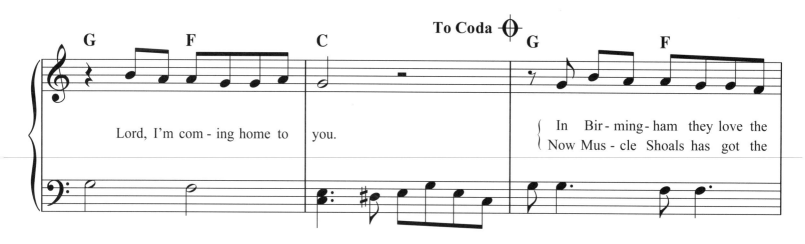

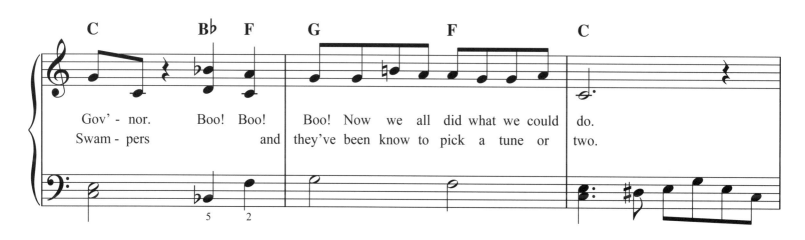

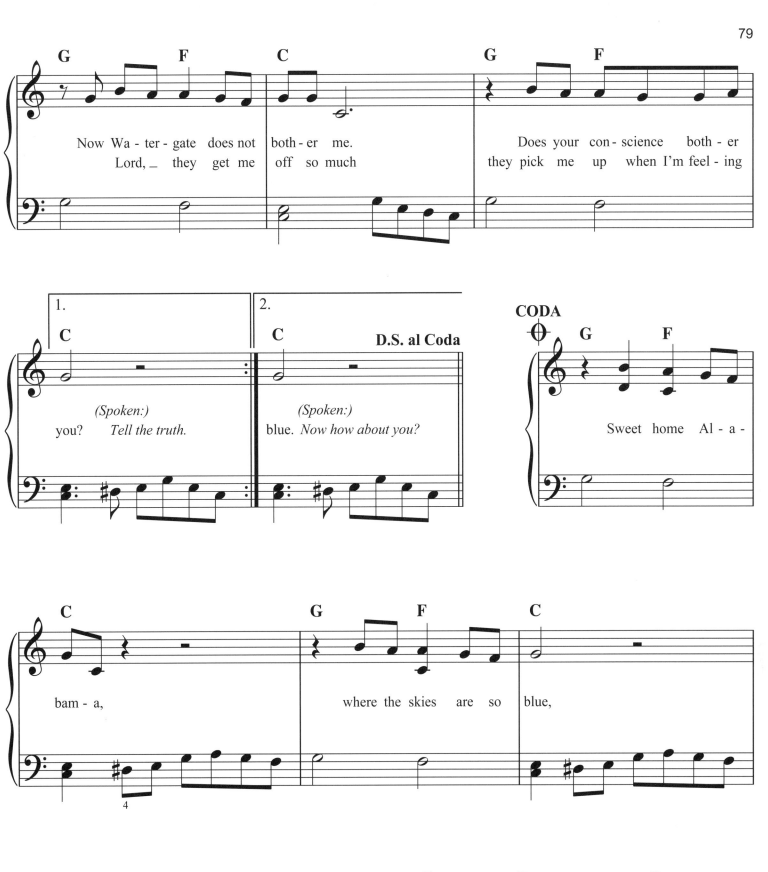

WE ARE FAMILY

Words and Music by NILE RODGERS
and BERNARD EDWARDS

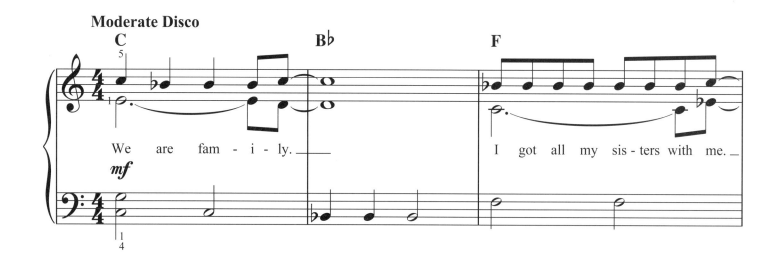

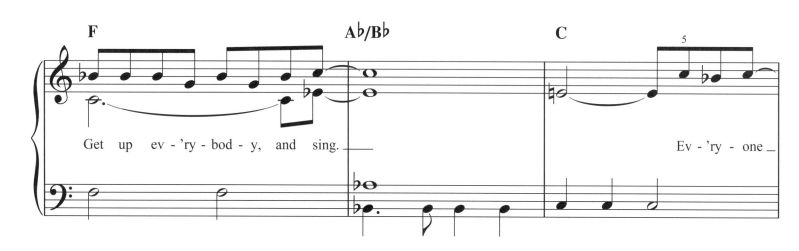

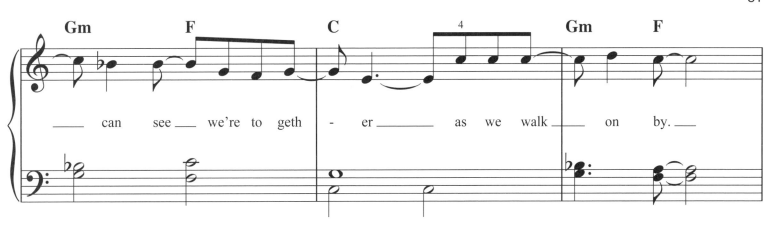

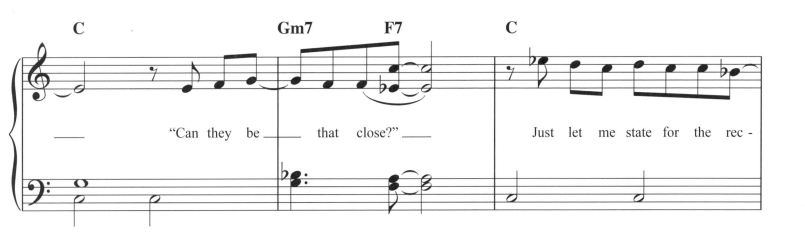

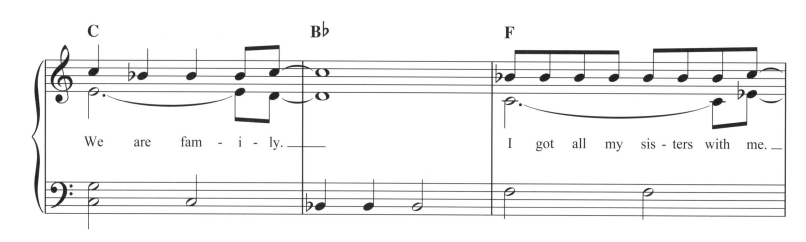

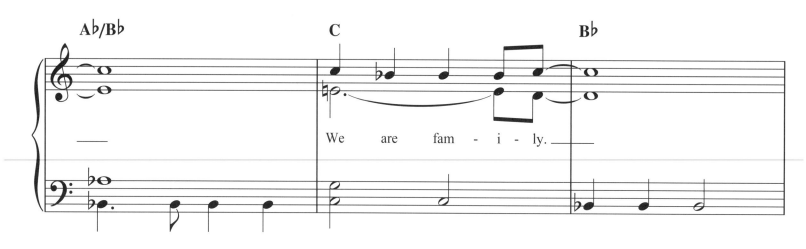

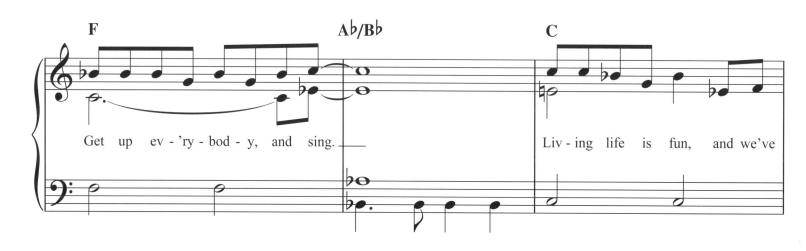

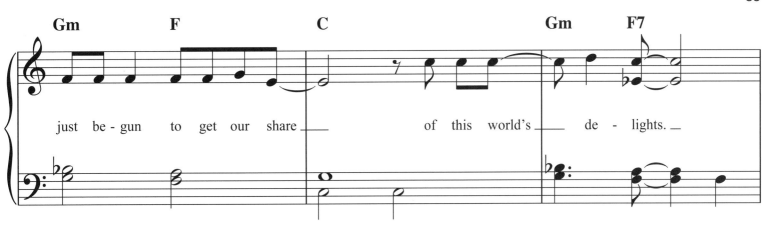

just be-gun to get our share ___ of this world's ___ de - lights. ___

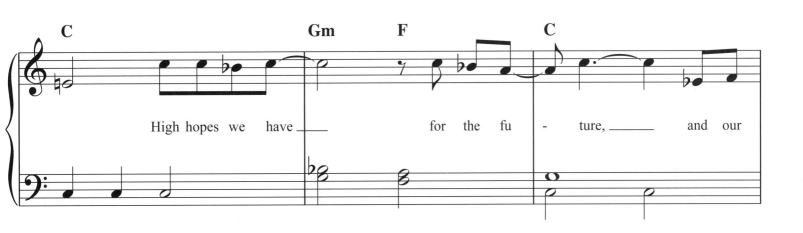

High hopes we have ___ for the fu - ture, _____ and our

goal's in sight. ___ No, we don't get de - pressed. ___ Here's what we call ___

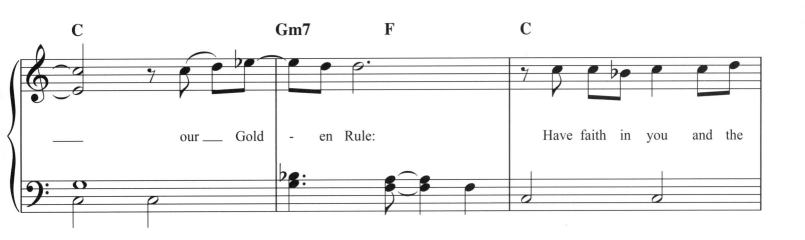

___ our ___ Gold - en Rule: Have faith in you and the

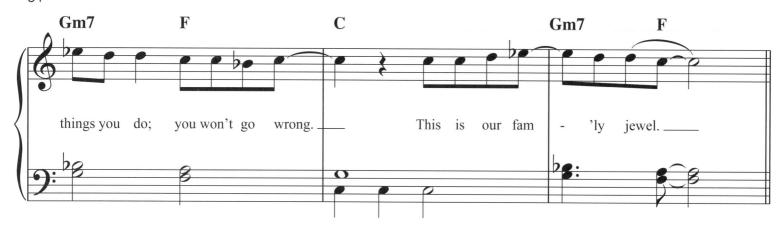

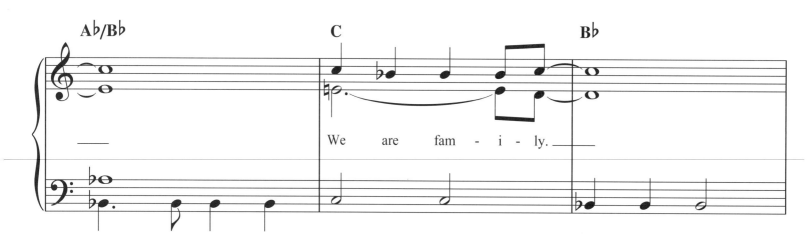

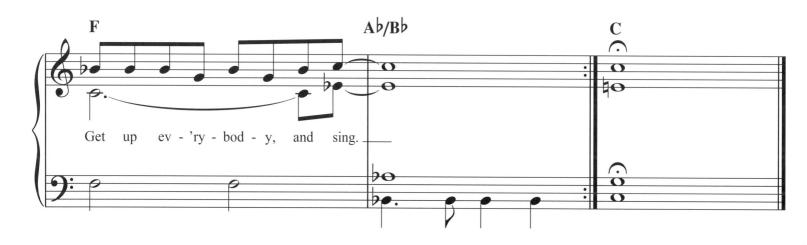

WHAT A WONDERFUL WORLD

Words and Music by GEORGE DAVID WEISS
and BOB THIELE

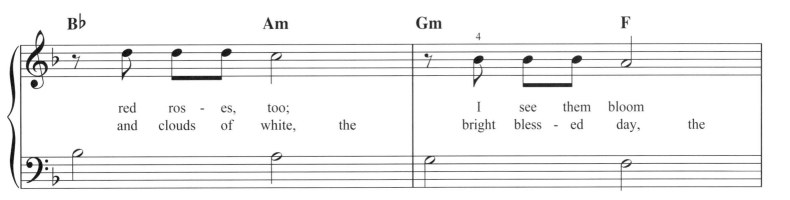

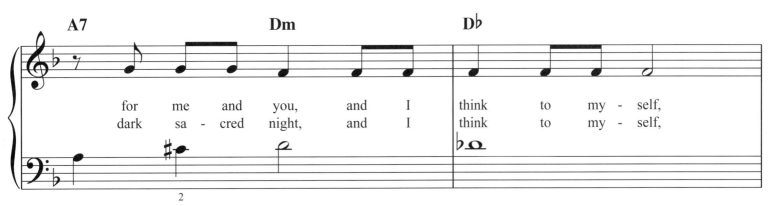

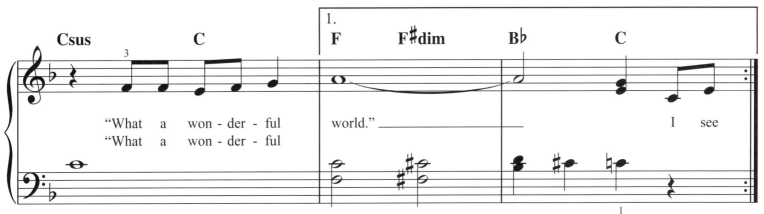

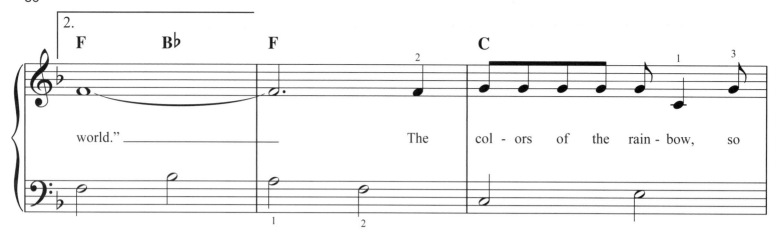

world." The col - ors of the rain - bow, so

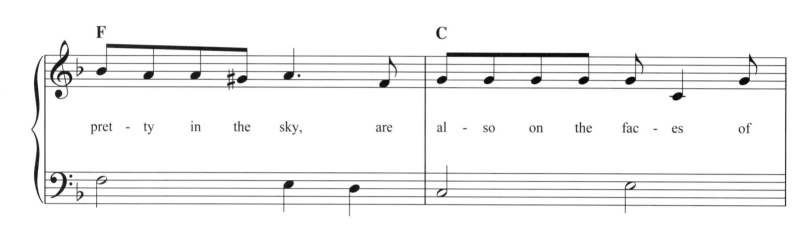

pret - ty in the sky, are al - so on the fac - es of

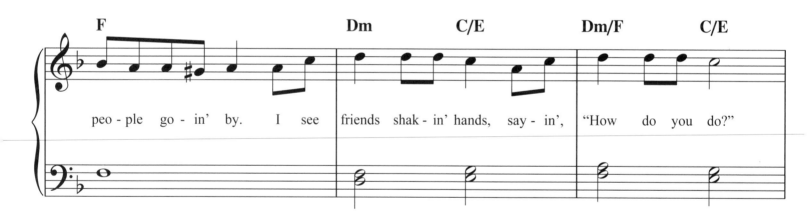

peo - ple go - in' by. I see friends shak - in' hands, say - in', "How do you do?"

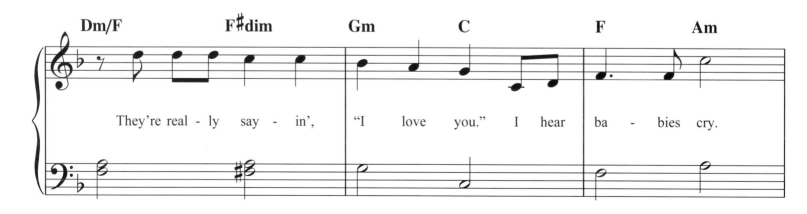

They're real - ly say - in', "I love you." I hear ba - bies cry.

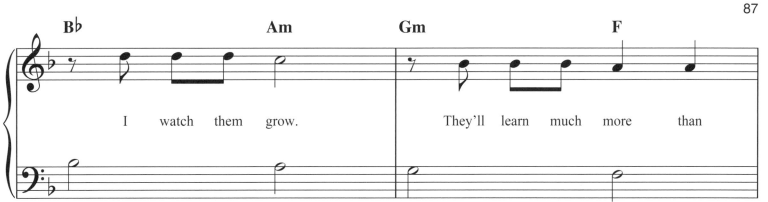

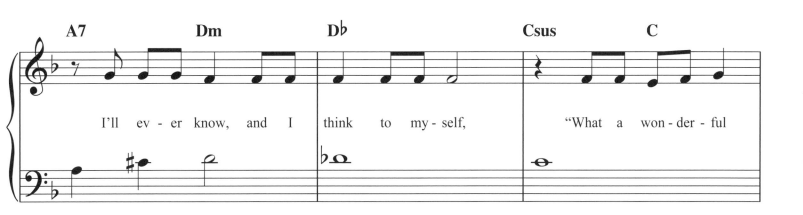

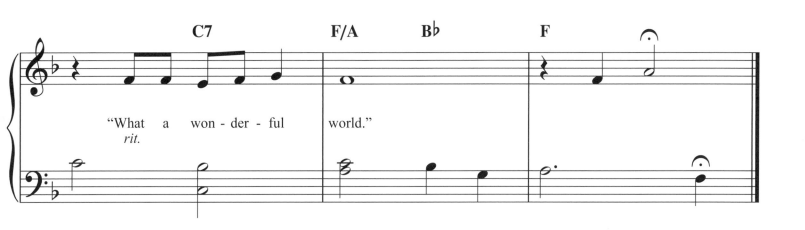

WILL YOU LOVE ME TOMORROW
(Will You Still Love Me Tomorrow)

Words and Music by GERRY GOFFIN
and CAROLE KING

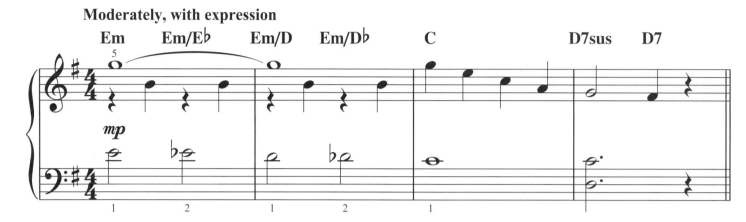

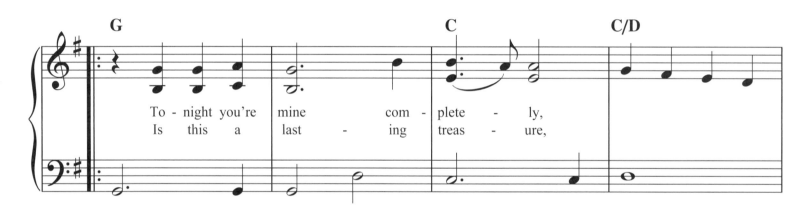

To - night you're mine com - plete - ly,
Is this a last - ing treas - ure,

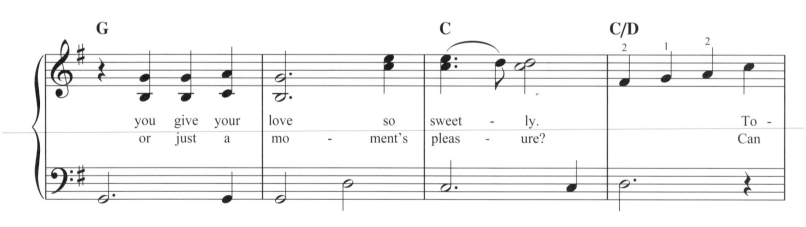

you give your love so sweet - ly. To -
or just a mo - ment's pleas - ure? Can

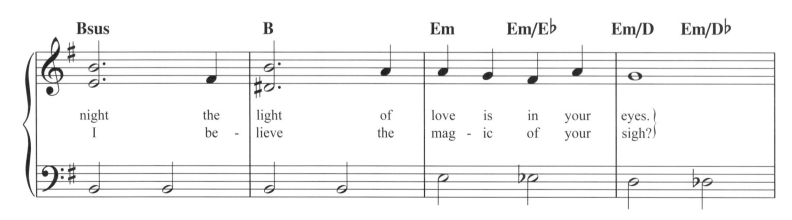

night the light of love is in your eyes.
I be - lieve the mag - ic of your sigh?

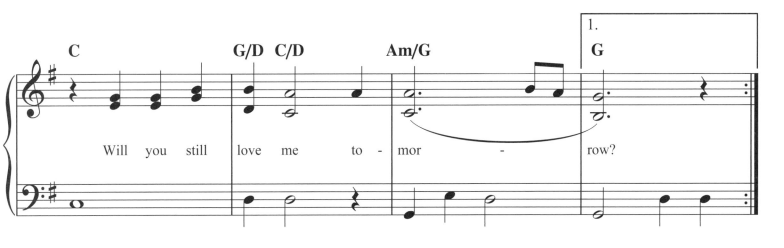

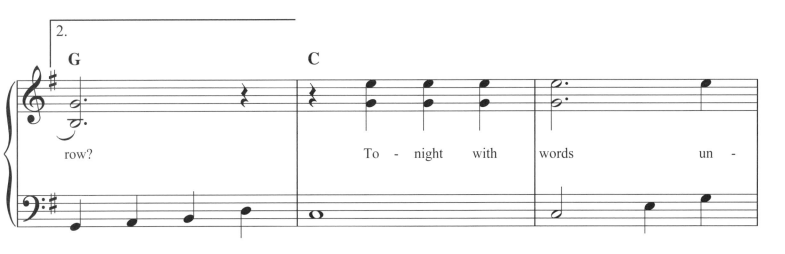

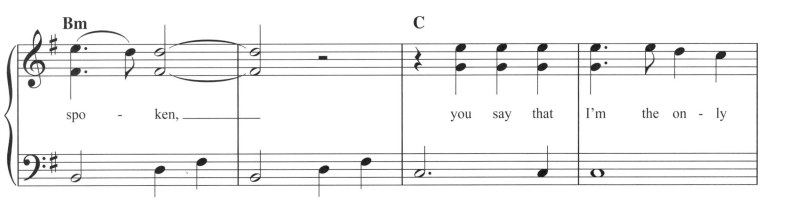

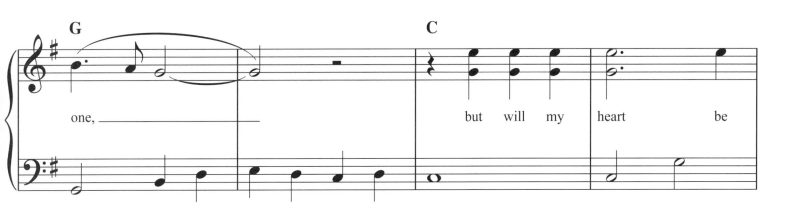

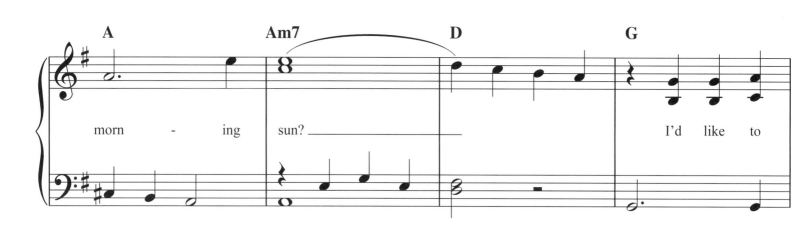

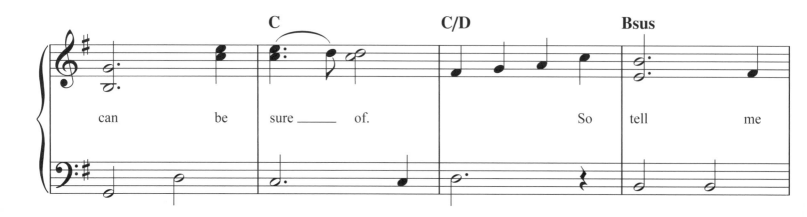

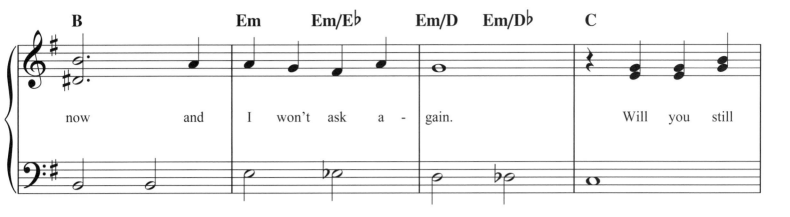

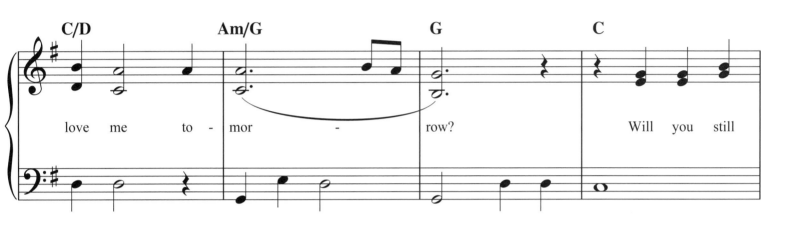

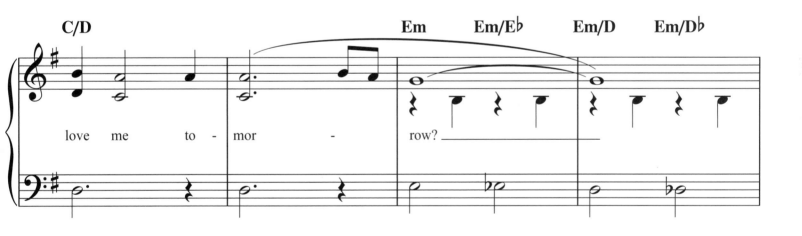

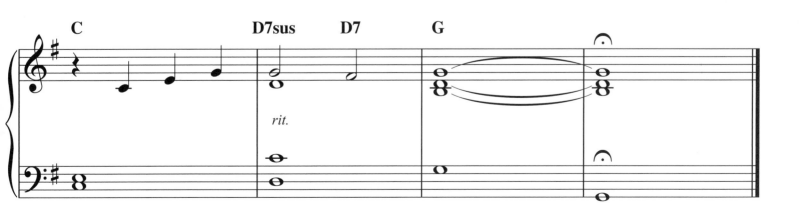

YESTERDAY

Words and Music by JOHN LENNON
and PAUL McCARTNEY

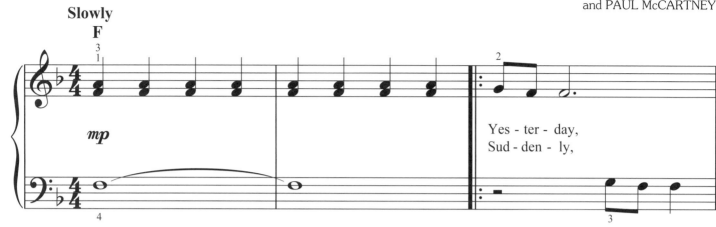

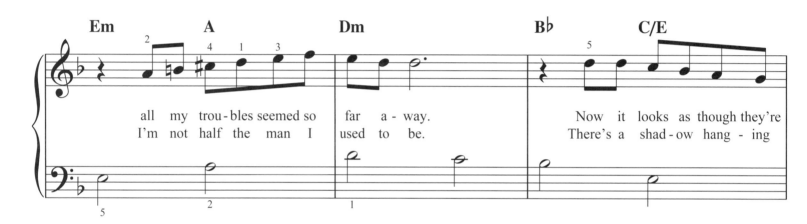

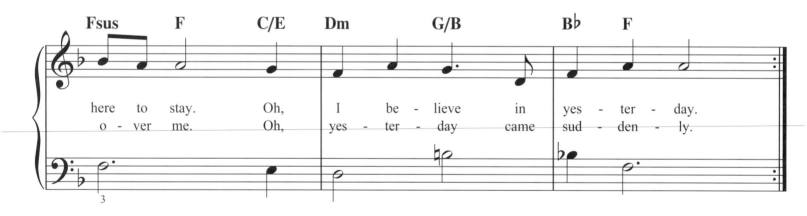

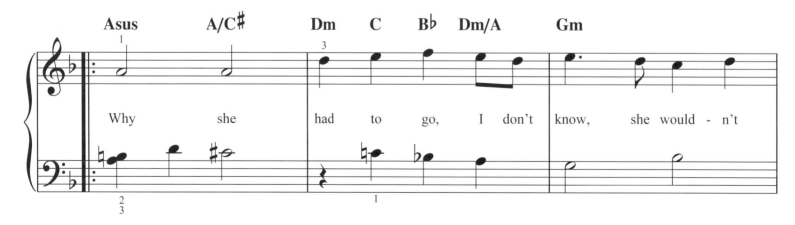

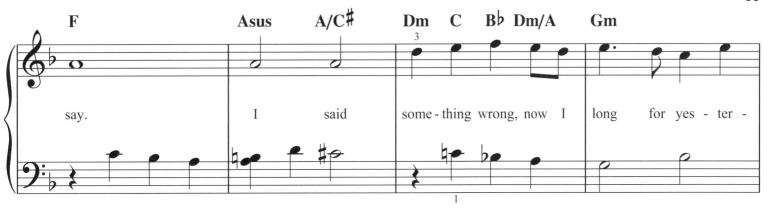

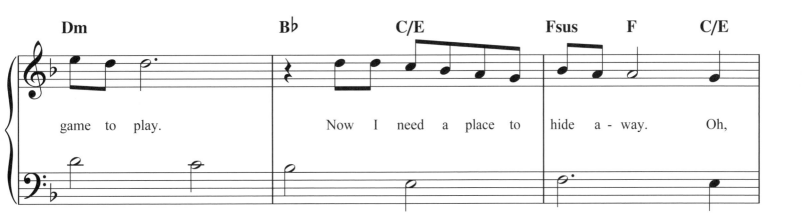

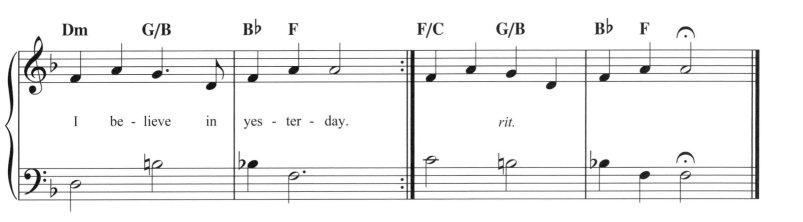

Y.M.C.A.

Words and Music by JACQUES MORALI,
HENRI BELOLO and VICTOR WILLIS

Young man, there's no need to feel down. __ I said,

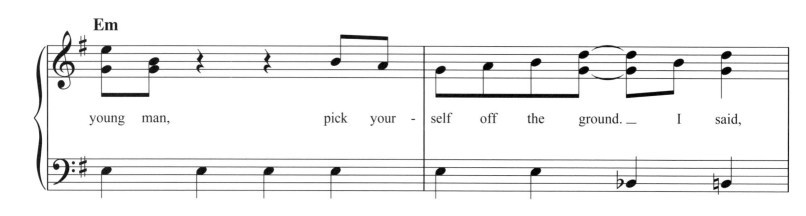

young man, pick your - self off the ground. __ I said,

young man, 'cause you're in a new town __ there's no need to __ be __

C G/B D/A   G

____ un - hap - py.   Young man,   there's a   place you can go, ___ I said,

Em

young man,   when you're   short   on   your   dough. ___ You   can

C   D/F♯   C/E   D

stay there   and I'm   sure you will find ___ man - y   ways   to ___ have ___

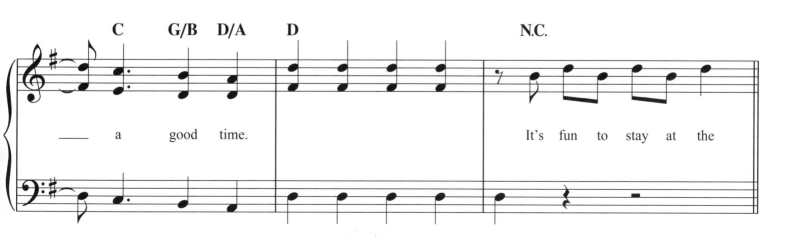

C G/B D/A   D   N.C.

___ a   good   time.   It's   fun   to stay   at the

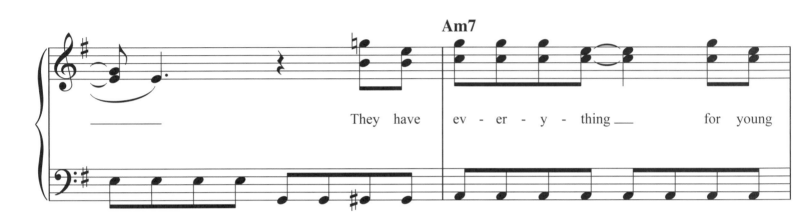

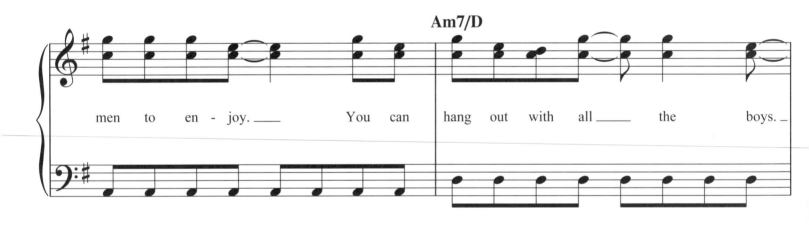

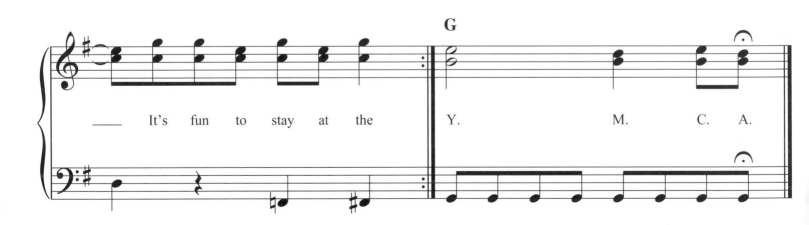